ESSAYS IN AESTHETICS

JEAN-PAUL SARTRE

ESSAYS IN AESTHETICS

Selected and translated by

WADE BASKIN

Essay Index Reprint Series

 BOOKS FOR LIBRARIES PRESS
FREEPORT, NEW YORK

INTERNATIONAL STANDARD BOOK NUMBER:

0-8369-1776-6

LIBRARY OF CONGRESS CATALOG CARD NUMBER:

73-117755

PRINTED IN THE UNITED STATES OF AMERICA

CONTENTS

INTRODUCTION

Jean-Paul Sartre's views on aesthetics are perhaps less controversial than his views on a number of other issues, particularly the human predicament. As a philosopher he has the dubious distinction of being a center of cult and controversy in Paris and of having most people who have heard of existentialism connect his name with the movement. As a novelist and dramatist he has popularized the notions stated systematically in his formidable masterwork *Being and Nothingness* and earned notoriety for the movement and its bizarre, pessimistic, perverse and bewildering appraisal of the human situation. As a typical French intellectual he has always exhibited an expanding omniscience that gives added emphasis to his statements on many vital issues, one of which is the place of art and artists in the human situation. Whether he speaks as philosopher, dramatist, novelist or critic, the ex-professor deserves a hearing.

Though he is the point of confluence of three post-Hegelian streams of thought — the Marxist, the existentialist and the phenomenological — and the product of traditional European thinking on aesthetics, ethics, metaphysics and politics, Sartre is profoundly and self-consciously individualistic in his interpretation of the human situation. He exploits the analytical tools of the Marxists and embraces their concern for action, but he disowns their politics. He rejects Kierkegaard's leap of faith but adopts his picture of man as a lonely, anguished creature in a chaotic universe. He discards Husserl's Platonism but adapts the latter's terminology to his own purposes. Add to this the rejection of Cartesian dualism and the adoption of Freudian insights, and the net result is an outlook and a style that produce in the reader a shock of recognition — a feeling that what he is reading is not something new but something long anticipated. Finally, though his tools and arguments evidence his indebtedness to his predecessors, his style and outlook are unmistakably contemporary.

Sartre approaches art with an open mind but seeks always to fit his findings into his philosophical scheme. The essays in this collection reveal his concern about fundamental issues relating to the nature of art and its place in the human situation as well as to the formation and function of the artist. And in questioning art he stirs the dust of metaphysical speculations: Is the artist "a man bent on imposing a human seal on space or a rock dreaming of human qualities?" Is our universe a "blind concatenation of causes and effects or the gradual unfolding, forever retarded, disconcerted and thwarted, of an Idea?" In these essays as in all his writings, we feel a spirit of dedication and a sincere desire on the part of the writer to change the life of the reader.

Four artists are discussed — two painters, one painter-sculptor, and one sculptor-painter. Each artist, because he embodies contradictions and confronts enigmas, presents a challenge to Sartre and affords him the opportunity to illustrate his theories about art. Tintoretto is the product of class contradictions and has to achieve self-affirmation through deceit. Giacometti is obsessed by his isolation in a world of things accessible only through their appearances and has to discover how to paint emptiness. Calder works on the borderland between freedom and control and has to discover how to imbue something immobile with movement. Lapoujade strives to reconcile creativity and beauty and must learn to "give to an infinitely divisible surface the indivisible unity of a whole."

Sartre's approach is doubly rewarding in that it affords new insights into the activities of both author and subject. In the case of Tintoretto, he offers a convincing refutation of legends that still survive and a brilliant case-study of an artist and his era. And in the case of his contemporaries, he shows how each has responded to the challenges of our own era. In addition to these new insights he provides us with a host of striking images and intimate asides: his definition of genius as "a conflict between a finite presence and an infinite absence"; his description of Tintoretto's paintings as a "passionate love affair" between a city and her rejected suitor; his allusions to the uniqueness of touch and the significance of the Other's look; his having to learn anew to live "at a respectable distance" from others after the end of World War II; his fright on boarding a plane as it relates to his love of beauty and his abhorrence of ugliness; his expressed hope that Giacometti will one day paint an illusion that will cause us to experience the "same shock that we feel on returning late and seeing a stranger walking toward us in the dark."

I wish here to express appreciation to those who have helped to prepare this collection of Sartre's essays on art. Professor Jean Lorson of the University of Oklahoma clarified for me several passages in the French texts. Four of my colleagues — Minnie Baker, Richard Bivins, Margaret O'Riley and Mildred Riling — shared the task of reading through the first draft of the translation: Professor Baker and Mr. Bivins paid particular attention to technical points posed by the translation of terms used in art; Dr. O'Riley read and corrected the first draft of the shorter essays; Professor Riling called attention to certain stylistic peculiarities of Sartre and suggested extensive revisions which were incorporated into the final version of the essay on Tintoretto. For their generous help and encouragement I am deeply appreciative.

WADE BASKIN

Southeastern State College

THE VENETIAN PARIAH*

Jacopo's Shenanigans

Nothing. His life is an enigma: A few dates, a few facts, and then the cackling of ancient writers. But courage: *Venice speaks to us.* Her voice is that of a perjured witness, now shrill, now whispering, always marked by periods of silence. Tintoretto's life story, the portrait painted during his lifetime by his native city, is tinged with unrequited animosity. The Doge's City reveals her contempt for the most celebrated of her sons. Nothing is stated outright; there are hints, suggestions, remarks made in passing. This inflexible hatred has the inconsistency of sand; it takes the form, not so much of outspoken aversion, as of coldness, moroseness, insidious ostracism. And this is just what we would expect. Jacopo fights a losing battle against a vast adversary, grows tired, surrenders, dies. That is the sum and substance of his life. We can study it in all its somber nakedness if for an instant we push aside the brushwood of slander that blocks our passage.

First, the birth of the dyer's son in 1518. Venice immediately insinuates that fate has marked him from the outset: "About 1530 the youth started to work in Titian's studio as an apprentice but was dismissed a few days later when the illustrious quinquagenarian discovered his genius." This anecdote reappears in book

*First published in *Les Temps Modernes* (November, 1957) under the title of *Le Séquestré de Venice*. (Translator's notes are indicated by an asterisk.)

after book with astounding regularity. It might be argued that it does little credit to Titian — and this is indeed the case — not *today*, at any rate, not in our eyes. But when Vasari reports it in 1567, Titian has been reigning for half a century, and nothing is more respectable than long impunity. Then too, according to the customs of his time, Titian has his own studio, where he is second only to God in the conduct of his affairs and has every right to dismiss an employee. In such circumstances his victim is presumed guilty; marked by fate, contagious perhaps, he is presumed to have the evil eye. Here for the first time the gilded legend of Italian painting is threatened by an ill-fated childhood. But the lesson to be learned from his alleged dismissal must come later. The voice of Venice never lies provided that we know how to interpret it; we can listen once our ears have been properly attuned. At this point we suspend judgment but call attention to the improbability of the facts.

That Titian was not good-natured is well known. But Jacopo was twelve. At twelve talent is nothing and anything will obliterate it; patience and time are required to mold nascent skill and change it into talent; no artist at the pinnacle of his fame — not even the most supercilious — would take umbrage at a small boy. But suppose that the master, jealous, dismissed his apprentice. That amounts to assassination of him. The curse of a national celebrity weighs heavily, very heavily. More especially as Titian lacks the candor to make known his true motives; he is king, he frowns and from this moment on all doors are closed to the black sheep. He is forever barred from the profession.

A blacklisted child is something of a rarity. Our interest quickens. We are eager to find out how he managed to overcome his handicap. Vain desire, for here the thread of the narrative breaks at the same time in every single book and we are confronted by a conspiracy of silence. No one will tell us what happened to him between the age of twelve and twenty. Some writers attempted to fill the void by imagining that he had learned the art of painting independently. But they were in an even better position than we to know that he could not have done so, for at the beginning of

2

the sixteenth century painting is still a complicated, rather ceremonious technique; unduly fettered by formulas and rites, it is a skill rather than an art, proficiency rather than knowledge, a set of procedures rather than a method. Professional rules, secret traditions — everything contributes toward making the apprenticeship a social obligation and a necessity. The biographers' silence betrays their embarrassment. Unable to reconcile the precocious notoriety of young Robusti and excommunication, they throw a veil of darkness on the eight years that separate the two. We can be certain that no one has rejected Jacopo; and since he has not perished from languor and scorn in his father's dye-shop, he must have worked normally and regularly in the studio of a painter about whom we know nothing except that *he was not* Titian. In closed, suspicious guilds hatred is retroactive; if the mysterious beginning of Jacopo's life seems a premonition of its mysterious end, if a curtain raised to show a disaster miraculously arrested is lowered on a disaster unattended by any miracle, this is because Venice rearranged everything afterwards to make his childhood consonant with his old age. Nothing happens and nothing ends; birth mirrors death and between the two lies scorched earth; everything is consumed by the curse.

We pass beyond these mirages and find our view unobstructed all across the horizon. An adolescent emerges, dashes away at high speed in search of glory. The year is 1539; Jacopo has left his patron to set up his own studio; he is now a *past master*. The young employee has won independence, fame, a clientele; now it is his turn to hire workers, apprentices. This much is certain: in a city filled with painters, where an economic crisis threatens to strangle the market, becoming a master at the age of twenty is the exception to the rule; merit alone is not enough, nor work, nor tact; one must also have a run of good luck. Everything is in Robusti's favor. Paolo Cagliari is ten, Titian sixty-two; between the unknown child and the old man who will surely die before long many good painters might be found, but only Tintoretto holds out the promise of excellence; in his generation, at any rate, he has no rival and therefore he finds the road before him open. He does in fact pursue

3

this road for several years: his commissions multiply, he enjoys the public's favor as well as that of patricians and intellectuals; Aretino deigns to congratulate him in person.* The young man is endowed with supernatural gifts which Providence reserves for adolescents who are to die, but he does not die and his woes begin: The old monarch Titian manifests a startling longevity, continuing all the while to vent his hatred on his young challenger and finally resorting to the malicious ruse of officially designating as his successor, to the surprise of no one, Veronese; Aretino's condescension turns to bitterness; critics lash out, censure, chide, castigate — in short, they behave like modern critics. This matters little so long as Jacopo retains the public's favor. But suddenly the wheel turns. At thirty, confident of his means, he asserts himself, paints *The Miracle of St. Mark* and puts himself, his whole self, into the painting. It is characteristic of him to astound, to strike hard and impose his will by surprise. In this instance, however, he will be the first to be caught off guard; his work dumbfounds his contemporaries but it also scandalizes them. He finds impassioned detractors but not impassioned defenders; behind the scenes we can detect a cabal: Frustration.[1] Face to face, united and separated by the same feeling of uneasiness, Venice and her painter contemplate but no longer understand each other. "Jacopo has not lived up to the promises of his adolescence," says the city. And the artist remarks, "To deceive them, all I had to do was reveal myself. So *I* was not what they loved!" Mutual grudges widen the gap between them, breaking one thread in the Venetian woof.

The pivotal year is 1548. *Before,* the gods are for him; *afterwards,* against. No great misfortunes are associated with his per-

*Because of the influence which he exercised over kings, diplomats and artists through his writings, Pietro Aretino (1492-1556) has been called the first journalist. Curiously, the amoral publicist whose services went to the highest bidder counted Titian among his devoted friends.

1. Ridolfi even maintains that the Scuola San Marco refused the canvas and that Tintoretto had to take it back to his studio.

sistent bad luck — just enough little ones to lead him to the brink of despair. The gods smiled on the child only to bring about the downfall of the man. Jacopo suddenly undergoes radical change and becomes the frantic, harassed outlaw, Tintoretto. *Before,* we know nothing about him except that he worked relentlessly, for fame is not easily acquired at the age of twenty. *Afterwards* his tenacity turns to rage; he wants to produce, to produce without ceasing, to sell, to crush his rivals by the number and dimensions of his canvases. There is a certain element of desperation in his forced effort, for until his death Robusti works against the clock without ever revealing whether he is trying to find himself through his work or to escape from himself through excessive activity. "Lightning Tintoretto" sails under a black flag, and for this swift pirate all means are fair, with a marked preference for unfair advantages. Disinterested whenever disinterest pays off, he lowers his eyes, refuses to name a price, repeats like a child, "It will be whatever you wish." But those Neapolitan rascals are in a better position than anyone else to know the value of their wares; they expect the customer to fleece himself through his generosity.

On other occasions he offers his merchandise at cost in order to close a transaction, only to make other more advantageous sales as a result of the initial emergency contract. On learning that the Crociferi are going to offer a commission to Paolo Cagliari, he feigns ignorance of everything and offers them his services. They essay a polite refusal: "Thank you, but we want something Veronese." And he: "Something Veronese?* Well and good. And who is going to do it?" Somewhat taken aback, they reply: "Why, we thought that Paolo Cagliari had been designated. . . ." And Tintoretto now expresses his amazement: "Cagliari? The idea is fantastic. I'll paint you something Veronese. And for less." Signed and sealed. He resorted to the same gambit twenty times, painting *in the style of* Pordenone, *in the style of* Titian, always for less.

How can he cut costs? That is the question that torments him.

*The spacious architectural quality of the paintings of Veronese (Paolo Cagliari, 1528-1588) is typical of his school.

5

One day he finds the contemptible but ingenious answer that will wreck a tradition. The masters are accustomed to having their canvases copied; their studios execute replicas and sell them at inflated prices, thereby creating a second market for their paintings. To win over their clientele, Jacopo will offer them *better paintings for less.* He eliminates sketches; he will allow others to draw their inspiration from his canvases but not to copy them; through simple, invariable procedures his collaborators will produce something new but not original. They will need only to rearrange the composition, put the left on the right and the right on the left, substitute an old man for a woman who can be used again in another context. Such operations require some training but no more time than simple copying. Tintoretto candidly proclaims: "In my studio one can acquire an original work for the price of a reproduction."

When his canvases are spurned, he gives them away. On May 31, 1564, at the Scuola San Rocco the Brotherhood decides to beautify its conference hall by placing a painting in the central oval of the ceiling. Paolo Cagliari, Jacopo Robusti, Schiavone, Salviati and Zucearo are invited to submit sketches. Tintoretto bribes servants, obtains the exact measurements. He had already worked for the Brotherhood and I do not rule out the hypothesis that he found accomplices even within the *Banca e Zonta.* On the day set, each painter exhibits his sketch. When Robusti's turn comes, he electrifies them all. He climbs up a ladder, removes a section of pasteboard, and reveals above their heads a dazzling painting, already in place, already finished. Pandemonium. "A drawing is easily misunderstood," he explained. "While I was about it, I preferred to see it through. But if my work is displeasing to you, gentlemen, I will give it to you. Not to you, but to San Rocco, your patron, who has done so much for me." This forced their hand and the rascal knew it, for the rules of the Brotherhood prohibited their refusing religious donations. All that remained was for them to make the episode a matter of record in the Scuola: "On this day the undersigned Jacopo Tintoretto, painter, presented to us a painting; he asks no remuneration, promises to complete the work if requested to do so, and states that he is satisfied with

6

it." And the undersigned wrote in his turn: *"Io Jachomo Tentoretto pintor contento et prometo ut supra."*

Satisfied? Why not? His gift spreads panic among his competitors, opens to him every door of the Scuola, places its vast, barren walls at the mercy of his brush and finally brings him an annual pension of a hundred ducats. So satisfied is he, in short, that he repeats the gambit in 1571. At the Doge's Palace this time, Authorities, wishing to commemorate the battle of Lepanto, organize a contest. Instead of a sketch Tintoretto brings a canvas and presents it as a gift. It is accepted with gratitude; shortly thereafter he sends his bill.

In his base but charming shenanigans one is tempted to see, perhaps, a trait attributable more to morals than to character. We might with some degree of accuracy say that ostentation was characteristic not of Tintoretto but of his century. If an attempt were made to condemn him on the basis of these anecdotes, I know everything that might be said in his defense. The most telling argument is that no one at that time could *work for himself*. Today paintings are in demand; then painters were for sale. They lined the market place like the *bracchiante* in the southern towns; buyers came, examined all of them, singled out one and took him to their church, their *scuola* or their *palazzo*. Artists had to make themselves available, to advertise themselves as our directors do, to accept just any work in the same way that our directors accept just any scenario in the foolish hope of using it to display their talents. Everything was under contract: the subject, number, quality, and sometimes even the attitude of the figures, and the dimensions of the canvas; these were complemented by restrictions imposed by traditions relating to religion and to taste. Their clients had their moods just as our producers have their whims. And their clients — alas! — they, too, had their sudden inspirations; at their bidding, everything had to be reworked. In the palace of the Medici, Benozzo Gozzoli was for a long time knowingly tortured by idiotic patrons; and we need only compare Tintoretto's *Paradise* in the Louvre with the one in the Doge's Palace to understand the magnitude of the pressures to which he was subjected. Intransigence,

7

rejection of compromise, the superb choice of misery were out of the question since the artist had to provide for his family and keep his studio in operation, as present-day machines are. In sum, he had to renounce painting or to paint according to instructions. No one can blame Tintoretto for wishing to become rich. As a matter of fact, toward the middle of his life he was never out of work, never lacked money. This utilitarian artist followed the principle that nothing is done for nothing, that painting would be a mere pastime unless it produced some income. At long last, as we shall see, he will buy a comfortable plebeian house in a residential district. This purchase will crown his career, exhaust his savings, leave the Robusti children with only a ludicrous heritage to divide: the contents of his studio, a diminishing clientele, and the house itself, which is passed on to the oldest son, then to his son-in-law. Twelve years after the death of her husband, Faustina recalls bitterly that he left his family in need; she has every reason to complain, for the deceased had his own way. He liked money, of course, but in the American way. He saw in it nothing more than the external sign of success. At the bottom, this contract chaser sought only one thing: the means of practicing his craft. There is also an element of justice in his shenanigans, for they would be inconceivable without his professional talent, hard work, and speed. His speed gives him an advantage, for to paint a good picture he requires only the time taken by others to make bad sketches.

Furthermore, if he plagiarized Veronese, the latter repaid him in kind. Their reciprocal borrowings must be viewed through the eyes of their contemporaries. For many of their contemporaries the greatest painters are those who have met the test of certain social criteria; they are personalities defined by collective judgment. We are interested in a particular painting at first, and then in the particular man who painted it; we hang Matisse on our walls. But contrast our view with that of the *Crociferi*: they were not interested in Cagliari; they wanted a certain style that appealed to the senses, trifles, inoffensive and harmonious pomp; they knew a trademark, a slogan. A painting signed Veronese is certain to please. That is

8

what they wanted, nothing else. Cagliari could produce better works and proved it when he painted his *Terrible Crucifixion,*[1] but he was too shrewd a businessman to squander his genius. Under such conditions we could hardly blame Tintoretto for appropriating at times a style that belonged exclusively to no one. After all, he made an honest proposal: "You want something trite and lifelike? I will provide it."

I am aware of the tastes of his age. My aim here is not to judge him but to determine whether his age could identify itself with him without discomfort. And on this point the evidence is explicit: his conduct shocked his contemporaries and turned them against him. A little disloyalty would perhaps have been tolerated, but Tintoretto went too far; throughout Venice a single complaint was voiced: "He goes too far!" Even in that commercial city such shrewdness in commerce is unique. At the Scuola San Rocco, when he stole their commission, his colleagues barked so loudly that he felt obliged to appease them: the establishment had other ceilings and walls, the work had only begun; as for him, now that his gift had been accepted, he would disappear, leaving the field open to the most worthy of them. His unfortunate rivals soon discover that he is lying like a pagan, for the Scuola will become his fief, and as long as he lives, no other painter will ever cross the threshold. They had surely not waited for this occasion to begin hating him. It is worth noting, however, that the scandal occurs in 1561 and that the first *Life* of Tintoretto appears in 1567. The shortness of the interval between the two events further enlightens us concerning the origin and significance of the ugly rumors collected by Vasari*. Calumnies on the part of jealous rivals? They were all extremely jealous of each other; why, then, are calumnies heaped on Robusti alone unless he is the "foul smell" of the artists, unless he represents in the eyes of each and all the collective

---

1. It is in the Louvre. The irony is that he was inspired by the *real* Robusti.

*The celebrated painter, architect and biographer published his *Lives of Excellent Painters, Sculptors, and Architects* in 1550. The date generally given for the revised edition is 1568.

9

and magnified faults of his fellow men? Furthermore, even his clients seem shocked by his conduct. Not all of them, no. But he has made numerous enemies in high places. Zammaria de Zigninoni, a member of the San Rocco Brotherhood, promises fifteen ducats for decorative works under the express condition that Jacopo not be given the commission. The records of the Brotherhood suggest, moreover, that the *Banca e Zonta* held a few tense and somewhat unceremonious meetings in the Scuola in connection with the restricted donation and Jacopo's gambit; an agreement was reached but Zigninoni kept his ducats. Nor do the officials always seem kindly disposed toward him. In 1571, Tintoretto contributes his *Battle of Lepanto;* in 1577 the painting is destroyed by fire; when the question of replacing it arises, he has every reason to believe that the government will call on him. Not at all. He is deliberately passed over and preference is shown instead to the mediocre Vincentino. It might be argued that his canvas had met with disfavor. But that is hardly plausible, for Jacopo always treads softly when working for the officials; he "paints like Titian," disguising his own style. Besides, after 1571 the government gave him several commissions. No, the Venetian authorities have no intention of depriving themselves of his services; they simply want to punish him for his rascality. In short, there is unanimity: he is a disloyal colleague, a maverick painter, and there is bound to be something unsavory about him since he is without friends. Sweet troubled souls who use the dead to edify the living and especially yourselves, try if you will to find in his excesses the glittering proof of his passion. The fact is that passions are as diverse as people: ravenous and contemplative, dreamy and practical, abstract, dawdling, apprehensive, rash — a hundred others. I will call Tintoretto's passion practical, apprehensive-recriminatory and ravenous-rash. The more I reflect on his ludicrous gambits, the more I become convinced they were born of an ulcerated heart. What a nest of vipers! There we find everything: the delirium of pride and the folly of humility, chained ambition and unchained confusion, harsh rebukes and persistent bad luck, the goad of success and the lash of failure. His life is the story of an opportunist tormented by fear; it has a

10

healthy, sprightly beginning; the offensive is well staged until the hard blow of 1548; after this the rhythm quickens, goes out of control, lights the fires of hell. Jacopo will fight on until the time of his death, knowing that he will not win. Opportunism and anguish, those are the two biggest vipers. If we wish truly to know him, we must have a closer look at them.

THE PURITANS OF THE RIALTO

No one is a cynic. To be discouraged in the absence of discouragement is the diversion of saints. Only up to a certain point, however, for these chaste and generous creatures stigmatize their lechery and denounce their avarice. If they discover their real gangrene — saintliness — they look for justification, like all guilty creatures. *Tintoretto* is no saint; he knows that everyone in town condemns his conduct; he persists only because he thinks that he is right and they are wrong. And let no one come up and say that he is aware of his genius, for a genius — this is ironical but true — knows his courage but not his worth. Nothing is more wretched than sullen temerity that reaches for the moon and writhes in defeat; first comes pride, without proofs or pedigrees; when it matures into madness we can call it genius if we choose, but I fail to see that very much is gained thereby. No, to justify his piracy Tintoretto pleads neither limited originality nor unlimited aspirations. He defends his rights, claiming that he has been wronged whenever a commission goes to one of his colleagues. Left to himself, he would have covered every wall in the city with his paintings; no *campo* would have been too vast, no *sotto portico* too obscure for him to illuminate. He would have covered the ceilings, people would have walked across his most beautiful images, his brush would have spared neither the façades of the palaces that line the Canale Grande nor the gondolas, nor perhaps the gondoliers. The man imagines that he was born with the privilege of transforming his city single-handed, and a good case can be drawn up in his favor.

When he begins his apprenticeship painting is on the wane. In Florence the crisis is manifest; Venice, as always, is silent or hypocritical, but we know for a certainty that the authentic Rialtan sources of inspiration have dried up. At the end of the fifteenth century the city is deeply affected by the passing of Antonello da Messina. His death marks a turning point; afterwards painters are imported. I am not saying that they are brought in from distant regions but simply that the most famous painters come from the mainland: Giorgione, from Castelfranco; Titian, from Pieve di Cadore; Paolo Cagliari and Bonifazio dei Pitati, from Verona; Palma Vecchio, from Sarinalta; Girolamo Vecchio and Paris Bordone, from Treviso; Andrea Schiavone, from Zara; and others still. As a matter of fact, this aristocratic republic is primarily a technocracy and has always been bold enough to recruit specialists from far and wide and clever enough to treat them as her own. Moreover, this is the time when the Republic of Venice, checked at sea and threatened by coalitions on the continent, turns to the hinterlands and tries through conquests to assert her might. Most of the new immigrants are from annexed territories. Venice betrays her anxiety by importing artists on a massive scale. When we recall that the artists of the Quattrocento were for the most part born inside the walls of the city or in Murano, we cannot suppress the notion that after the extinction of the Vivarini and Bellini families and after the death of Carpaccio, the resurgence of her generations of artists would not have been possible without a blood transfusion.

Painting is like all the other crafts in that the patriciate is responsible for facilitating the immigration of good artisans and — to prove what might be called their cosmopolitan chauvinism — for making the Republic of the Doges into a melting pot. In the eyes of his distrustful and jealous aristocracy, foreigners make the best Venetians; their adoption of Venice is proof of inspiration just as aloofness signals a weak character. We can be sure that the local artisans did not look upon the newcomers in the same way. Why should they? For them the newcomers represent foreign competition. They are tactful enough not to complain, and they carry on as if nothing were wrong; but there are conflicts, inescapable evidences of tension, charges and countercharges stemming from wounded pride. Forced to bow to the technical superiority

13

of the alien settlers, the natives hide their humiliation by expanding their prerogatives. They agree to take second place to the most skilled, to the most expert, but only in return for a sacrifice: their birthright must remain intact. Only a Rialtan can claim Venice as his own; while Germans are better glaziers, they can never boast that they are true Venetians. Before their disappearance the great painters of the Quattrocento had the bitter experience of seeing the public turn away from them and bestow their favors on young intruders who scorned them. For example Titian, the outsider, leaves one of the Bellini brothers for the other — Gentile for Giovanni — in pursuit of still another outsider, Antonello, the meteor that rent the sky and the water of the lagune twenty years earlier. Tiziano Vecellio has no need of Giovanni; what he seeks in him is a reflection; he proves this by soon abandoning the master of the disciple and joining Giorgione's school, for the third alien seems to the second to be the true heir to the first. Tiziano and Giorgio belong to the same generation: the pupil may even be older than the teacher. Did the Bellini brothers realize on that day that they had served their time? And what did Giovanni's true disciples say? And the others, the last representatives of the Murano school, what did they think? Many of them were youngsters or men still in their prime; the influence of Antonello da Messina had reached all of them through Giovanni Bellini; colors and light came from Messina, but their acclimatization was effected by Giovanni; through him they had become Venetian. The young artists staked their honor on remaining faithful but were strangled by their fidelity. They did their best to adapt to new conditions without abandoning the rather crude techniques that they had been taught, but to do so was to accept mediocrity. They must have felt bitter resentment on seeing two young intruders join forces, break with the indigenous tradition, rediscover the secrets of a Sicilian, and effortlessly carry painting to its highest perfection. Giovanni still reigns, however, and the fame of this admirable artist spreads throughout northern Italy. The barbarian invasion begins during his latter years and triumphs after his death in 1516.

At the height of the invasion, the greatest painter of the century is born in the heart of the occupied city, in an alley on the Rialto. A somber plebeian pride, always humiliated, always rebuffed, constantly in waiting, seizes upon the opportunity, infiltrates the heart of the sole Rialtan with a remnant of talent, emboldens and inflames it. We recall that he springs directly from neither the working class nor the bourgeoisie. His father is a successful artisan, a member of the petty bourgeoisie, who takes pride in not working for others. As the son of a working man Jacopo would perhaps have remained the obscure collaborator of an artist; as the son of an independent craftsman, however, he has to become a master or a failure. He will pass through the ranks but is prevented by his class and family status from stopping along the way. That he fails to leave good impressions in the studio where he serves his apprenticeship is understandable, for his aim on entering the studio was to leave it as soon as possible to reclaim the place already reserved for him in the social hierarchy. Then, too, Schiavone (or Bordone or Bonifazio dei Pitati — they are all the same) must have looked upon him as an intruder while Jacopo considered his master an alien or a thief. The Little Dyer is a *native* and Venice is his birthright. Had he been a mediocre painter, he would have remained modest and resentful; but he is brilliant and knows it, and he will take second place to no one. Aliens, in the eyes of a Rialtan, have nothing to protect them other than their professional worth; if Jacopo outshines them as a painter, they will have to disappear, even if this means their assassination. No one paints or writes without a mandate; would anyone dare if "*I* were not the Other"?* Jacopo is given a mandate by a toiling population to redeem through his art the privileges of a purebred Venetian. That explains his unscrupulous conduct. Popular recri-

---

*"The Other" occupies a central position in the existential world: "The Other is not only the one whom I see but the one *who sees me*" and makes it possible for me to "recognize that I *am*" as he sees me; I do not choose to be what I am for the Other, "but I can try to be for myself what I am for the Other, by choosing myself as I appear to the Other." Quoted from "The Other and His Look" in Justus Streller's *To Freedom Condemned* (New York; Philosophical Library, 1960).

mination fills his heart with an abiding desire to reassert a claim; he has been given the task of winning recognition of his rights; whoever champions such a just cause can use any means to succeed—he will show no mercy, give no quarter. His misfortune results from the fact that his struggle against the undesirables brings him into conflict with the patriciate and its policy of assimilation of foreigners in the name of the indigenous artisans. When he shouted in the streets, "Veronese to Verona!" it was the government that he was calling in question. Realizing this, he hesitates, then resumes his obstinate course, exhibiting a curious mixture of flexibility and inflexibility. As a prudent subject of a police state he always gives in, or pretends to; as an *indigenous* citizen of the most beautiful of all cities, his arrogance is boundless; he can even be servile without losing his ankylosis of pride. Everything is to no avail. His schemes against those protected by the aristocracy are thwarted by his impatience or by his incurable bluntness, or they backfire. Now we see the rancor of the Republic in a new light. The subject asks essentially only for what would probably have been accorded him, but his perverse submissiveness nettles the authorities, and they consider him a rebel. Or at the very least they are suspicious of him, and their suspicions are well founded. The consequences of his impetuousness are worth examining.

First, the studied and almost sadistic violence which I will call lack of self-restraint. Born among the underlings who endured the weight of a superimposed hierarchy, he shares their fears and their tastes; we find their prudence even in his presumptuousness. His neighbors, alert, courageous, somewhat suspicious of outsiders, have helped him to establish a system of values, shown him the dangers that life holds in store, pointed out the hopes that are permitted and those that are prohibited. Specific, limited opportunities, a foreseeable destiny, a future already visible in its general outlines, being imprisoned inside a transparency like a tiny flower inside a glass paperweight — all this kills dreams. One desires only what is possible; this is a mitigating circumstance that enrages fools and excites far-fetched but ephemeral ambitions. Jacopo's

16

ambition suddenly asserts itself. Bolstered by its virulence and diverse forms, it assimilates a minute pencil of light, its possibilities. Or rather, nothing is *possible*. There is a means and there is an end in view, which is the prescribed task; one can rise above the heaviest low-lying mists and touch the rigid, luminous membrane of the ceiling; there are other ceilings, membranes that grow progressively clearer and more delicate, and at the very top, perhaps, is the blue of the sky. But what does this matter to Tintoretto; each has his own soaring range and his own habitat. Tintoretto knows that he is talented; he has been told that his talent is his capital. By putting his capacities to the test he will capitalize on them and provide himself with an adequate income. And so we see him totally mobilized for a long life, prepared always to exploit the vein even to the point of depletion of both mine and miner. At about the same time another slave to work, Michelangelo, is undertaking projects only to desert them in disgust and leave them unfinished. Tintoretto *always* finishes things with the terrible application of a man bent on finishing his statements come what may; even death stood aside for him at San Giorgio, where it allowed him to apply the finishing touches to his last canvas, or at least to give final instructions to his collaborators. Never during his entire life did he allow himself an indulgence, a dislike, a preference, or even the comfort of a dream. During periods of exhaustion he must have repeated to himself this principle: "To refuse a commission is to hand it over to my colleagues."

He has to produce at any cost. Here the will of a man and that of a city coalesce. A hundred years earlier Donatello had scolded Uccello for sacrificing creativity to experimentation and for carrying the love of painting to the point of ceasing to paint pictures;* but that was in Florence, and the Florentine artists had just begun to risk experimentation with *perspective;* by applying to painted

*Paolo Uccello (1397-1475) first exhibited a heroic sense of design and helped to create the Renaissance superman. His rigorous application of linear perspective during a later period is generally assumed to represent a paradoxical return to Gothic traditions.

objects the laws of geometrical optics, they were trying to construct a new plastic space. Other times, other customs. In Venice, under the leadership of Titian, everyone shares the opinion that painting has just reached the peak of perfection, that further advances are impossible: Art is dead, long live life. The supreme barbarity begins with Aretino's foolish statements: "How realistic it is! How true to life! *You would never believe it is painted!*" In short, it is time for painting to disappear in the face of *realizations;* inspired merchants want something beautiful and useful. A work ought to please the lover of art, dazzle Europe with the pageantry of the Republic, awe the people. And still today we stand in awe, we the little tourists, before the Venetian cinemascope and prattle about one of Titian's realizations, one of Paolo Cagliari's productions, one of Pordenone's performances, one of Vecention's stagings. Jacopo Robusti shares the prejudices of his age, and our experts stress the point. How many times have I heard them say, "Tintoretto, bah! Just like the movies." And still, no one else in the world, either before or after him, has carried so far the passion for research. With Titian, painting flowers and dies, a victim of its own perfection; Jacopo sees in its death the necessary condition for a resurrection: everything is to have a new beginning, to be done over — a theme to which we shall return. But — and this is his major contradiction — he will never allow his experiments to restrict his productivity. So long as there remains in Venice one barren wall, the painter's task is to cover it; morals prohibit transforming a studio into a laboratory. Art is in its entirety a serious profession and a battle to the death against intruders. Like Titian, like Veronese, Jacopo will produce exquisite cadavers. With one difference: his cadavers are racked by fever, and we do not know at first whether this is the aftermath of life or the onset of putrefaction. And if the comparison with movie-making is pressed, he resembles the cinematographer in *this* respect: he accepts imbecile scenarios but imbues them with his obsessions. He has to fool the buyer, to give him something for his money; the buyer will have his Catherine, his Theresa, his Sebastian; for the same price he will have on the same canvas, if there is sufficient room, his wife and his brothers. But underneath it all, behind the sumptuous and banal façade of the *realization,* he pushes forward his experimentation. Each of his great works has a double meaning; its strict utilitarianism disguises an unending quest. Fitting his research into the frame of the paid commission, he is obliged to revolutionize painting even while respecting the stipulations of his client. Such is the inner motivation of his excessive activity, and such will later be the reason for his perdition.

He also has to win commissions. We have already seen that he succeeds. But let us re-examine his actions; now they will appear in a new light. Tintoretto's rebellion has various repercussions. Having rebelled against the politics of the melting-pot, he is forced to infringe upon corporate regulations or practices. The government, unable to eliminate competition and aware of its advantages, takes pains to channel it through contests. The powerful and the rich, if their taste is the deciding factor, will preserve public order by practicing bland protectionism in the form of directed competition.

Are they sincere? Doubtless, and all would be perfect if we were certain of their abilities but we have only their word. Sometimes harmony reigns — and then they choose Vincentino. Tintoretto always avoids their contests. Does he deny their competence? Certainly not! He simply refuses them the right to treat a native in the same way as an intruder. But contests do exist, and by shunning them, our rebel is trying deliberately to destroy protectionism. He is trapped in a corner. Since the officials pretend to base their judgment on merit, and since he challenges their right to judge him, he has either to renounce painting or to win recognition through the quality of his works. He loses no time in bringing his works to their attention. Seizing upon every opportunity, he takes his competitors by surprise, confronts his jurors with the accomplished fact, and utilizes all his cunning and speed, all the diligence of his collaborators in establishing a system of mass production which breaks every record and allows him to sell his canvases at rock-bottom prices, and at times to give them away. Two second-hand shops face each other on a Roman avenue; the shopkeepers, I imagine, have conspired to simulate a merciless struggle that will not cease until both shops are brought under a single proprietor; through their eternal confrontation the shop-windows suggest a tragic comedian bent on contrasting the two sides of his nature. One is covered with gloomy slogans: *"Prezzi disastrosi!"* The other contains multicolored placards which announce: *"Prezzi da ridere! da ridere! da ridere!"* This has been going on for years, and whenever I see the shops they make me think of Tintoretto. Had he chosen laughter or tears? Both, I think — depending on the client. We can even surmise that he chuckled privately and complained publicly that he was being robbed; in any case, in his studio, every day was like a year-end clearance sale, and clients were willing to meet the judicious prices set at his liquidation sales. Having set out to commission a medallion, they ended by turning over to him every wall in their house. He was the first to break the strained bonds of friendship within the confraternity. For this unlabeled Darwinist, colleague meant personal enemy, and he discovered before Hobbes the meaning of absolute competition: *Homo homini lupus.* Venice trembles. Unless a vaccine can be found to combat the virus Tintoretto, the good old corporate system will fall apart and all that remains will be smoldering antagonisms, molecular solitudes. The Republic condemns his new methods, brands them felonies, speaks of slipshod work, of cut-rate sales, of monopoly. Later, much later, other cities will honor his methods in another language, using terms like *struggle for life, mass production, dumping, trust,* etc. For a while this man of bad character will lose on one canvas all that he gains on another. Through hook or crook he will win commissions — but not acceptance. Through a strange reversal he, the *native,* the one-hundred-percent Rialtan, is an intruder, almost a pariah in his own city. The inevitable consequence is that he will perish unless he establishes a family. First, to stifle competition within his studio. This champion of liberalism reverses the Biblical precept; he will have others never do to him what he does to them. Moreover, he needs steadfast loyalty; outside collaborators can be frightened and discouraged by all the scandals circulated about him, and much time will be wasted if he has to reassure them.

None of the scandals will permanently damage his reputation. Why does he need disciples? He wants other hands, other pairs of arms, nothing more. From absolute competition to exploitation of the family — that is his course. In 1550 he marries Faustina dei Vescovi and immediately starts producing children. Just as he produces pictures: without let or hindrance. His brood has only one short-coming: there are too many girls. Too bad! He will put all of them except two in the convent: Marietta, whom he retains as his helper, and Ottavia, whom he marries to a painter. "Lightning Tintoretto" will persist until Faustina gives birth to two sons, Domenico and Marco. Before their arrival he has already begun to teach the craft to his oldest daughter, Marietta. A woman painter is something extraordinary in Venice. He must have been very impatient. Finally, around 1575, his operation is completed; the new staff includes Sebastiano Casser, his son-in-law, Marietta, Domenico and Marco. The symbol of a domestic association is the *domus* which protects and imprisons the group. At about the same date Jacopo buys a house, which he will never abandon. In this small lazaret the leper will live half-quarantined with his family, loving them more and more as he witnesses the swelling of the ranks of the *others* who hate him. On observing him *in his home*, at work, in his relations with his wife and children, we discover another side of his personality — that of the austere moralist. Was there not more than a trace of Calvinism in his life? We see here pessimism and work, the profit motive and devotion to the family. Human nature is vitiated by original sin; men are divided by self-interest. The Christian must seek salvation through his works; he must struggle for survival, labor unceasingly to improve the Earth that God has entrusted to him; he will find the mark of divine favor in the material success of his undertaking. As for the promptings of his heart, they should be reserved for the flesh of his flesh, for his children. Was Venice feeling the influence of the reformed Religion? We know that in the second half of the century there was in Venice an odd person, Fra Paolo Sarpi, who was popular among the patricians, hostile to Rome, and familiar with foreign Protestant movements. But in all probability the petty bourgeoisie knew nothing about the tendencies, discernible in certain intellectual quarters, that seemed vaguely to favor the Reform. It would be more accurate to say that the Republic reformed itself. And by Tintoretto's time this reform has been going on for a long time. Venetian merchants owe their living to credit; they can not accept the sentence pronounced by the Church on those whom it insists on labeling usurers, and they scorn Roman obscurantism in favor of science, especially when practical. The State has always affirmed the domination of civil authority and will not change its basic doctrine. The State has the upper hand over its clergy and, when Pope Pius V takes it upon himself to remove ecclesiastics from the jurisdiction of lay tribunals, the Senate pointedly refuses to recognize the removal. Furthermore, the government has many reasons for considering the Holy See a temporal and military power rather than a spiritual power. All this does not prevent the authorities from currying the Pope's favor, if the interest of the Republic is at stake, or pursuing heretics, or organizing a sumptuous feast in honor of St. Bartholomew to flatter a very Christian monarch. Tintoretto's pseudo-Calvinism is transmitted to him by his city; the painter unknowingly assimilates the benign Protestantism found at that time in every great capitalist stronghold.[1] The artist's position is then highly equivocal, especially in Venice. But let us press our advantage; this very ambiguity may well enable us to understand Jacopo's puritanical passion.

We read that "The Renaissance attributed to the artist the traits which Antiquity reserved for the man of action and which the Middle Ages had used to adorn its saints." This is not untrue, but to me the opposite observation seems at least equally true: "[During the sixteenth century] painting and sculpture were still looked upon as manual arts; all the honors were reserved for poetry. That explains the attempts to put the figurative arts on the

1. The very same one that inoculated Italian towns against the Lutheran sickness and encouraged Italy to carry out its own religious revolution under the name of Counter Reformation.

same footing with literature."[1] We know that Aretino, the Petronius of the poor and the Malaparte of the rich, was the arbiter of taste and elegance for the snobs of the Venetian patriciate and that Titian was honored by his friendship, for the artist, with all his fame, was not the poet's equal. And Michelangelo? He made the mistake of imagining that he was of noble birth, and this illusion ruined his life. As a youth he wanted to cultivate the humanities, to write, in the belief that a nobleman deprived of his sword could take up the pen without degrading himself. Forced to take up the chisel, he was never able to console himself. From his dais of shame he looked down upon sculpture and painting, deriving what empty, shriveled joy he could from feeling superior to what he was doing. Forced to remain silent, he sought to provide a language for the mute arts, to multiply allegories and symbols; he wrote a book on the ceiling of the Sistine Chapel and tortured marble to force it to speak.

What are we to conclude? Are the Renaissance painters heroes and gods, or are they manual workers? Everything is relative, depending on the clientele and the mode of remuneration. Or rather painters are primarily manual workers. They may become employees of the court or remain local masters. It is up to them to choose — or to be chosen. Raphael and Michelangelo are court appointees. Proud but dependent, they will be dumped in the street if on the slightest pretext they meet with disfavor; against this, the sovereign guarantees their fame. This sacred person accords to the elect a portion of his supernatural powers; the glory of his throne falls upon them like a ray of sunshine, and they reflect it upon the people; the divine right of kings gives painters divine rights. The result: daubers changed into supermen. Just who are these ordinary men whom a giant has snatched from the petty bourgeoisie and suspended between heaven and earth, these satellites whose borrowed splendor is overpowering? Are they anything other than ordinary men raised above humanity? They are heroes,

1. Eugenio Battista, in an excellent article on Michelangelo published in *l'Epoca* (August 25, 1957).

yes — intercessors, intermediaries. Today still, nostalgic republicans worship in them, under the guise of genius, the light from the dead star of Monarchy.

Tintoretto is of another ilk. He works for merchants, for officials, for parish churches. Not that he is uneducated. He was enrolled in school at the age of seven and probably ended his schooling at twelve, after he had learned to write and reckon; besides, and more important still, we would surely have to class as education the patient cultivation of the senses, of manual and mental faculties, and of the traditional empiricism still associated with studio painting around 1530. But he will never acquire the trappings of the court painters. Michelangelo writes sonnets; Raphael is supposed to have been versed in Latin; and Titian himself finally acquired a veneer through associating with intellectuals. Compared to these worldlings, Tintoretto seems like a dunce; he will never have the leisure or the taste for toying with ideas and words. He ridicules the humanism of men of letters. Venice has few poets and still fewer philosophers, but for him these are too many and he has nothing to do with any of them. Not that he shies away from them; he simply ignores them. He is willing to admit their social superiority. Aretino has every right to congratulate him with condescending benevolence; this high-ranking person has been *received* in Venice and is a member of the inner circle; patricians who would never dream of greeting a painter in the street invite him to their table. But does Tintoretto have to envy him, too? Does he have to envy him *because he writes?* To him the creations of the mind acquire an utterly immoral air because they are gratuitous. God placed us on the earth to earn our bread by the sweat of our brow; but writers do not sweat. Do they really work? Jacopo never opens a book with the exception of his missal; he would never be so foolish as to force his talent for the sake of competing with literature. His paintings include everything but *mean* nothing; they are as mute as the world. All that he really values, this son of an artisan, is physical effort, manual creation. What fascinates him in the profession of painting is that here professional ability is pushed to the point of prestidigitation and the delicacy of the

24

merchandise reduced to its quintessence. The artist is the supreme worker; he exhausts himself and his material in order to produce and sell visions.

That would not prevent him from working for princes if he liked them. He does not and that is the crux of the matter. They frighten him without inspiring him. He never tries to approach them or to make himself known to them. He seems to take pains to confine his reputation within the walls of Venice. During his whole life he left Venice only once, when he was in his sixties, to go just outside the city to Mantua. Even then he had to be begged to go. His clients wanted him to hang up his own canvases, but he refused to go without his wife. This stipulation not only affords proof of his conjugal sentiments; it leaves no doubt about his horror of travel. And it would be wrong to think that his Venetian colleagues share his horror, for they leave no road untraveled. A century earlier Gentile Bellini was sailing the seas. What adventurers! But Jacopo is a mole, happy only within the network of his molehills. Whenever he tries to imagine the outside world, he is gripped by terror; still, if he has a choice, he prefers to risk his skin rather than his paintings. He accepts foreign commissions — and for him anything beyond Padua is foreign — but does not solicit them. What a contrast between his frenzied behavior in the Doge's Palace, the Scuola San Rocco, the home of the Crociferi, and this indifference! He entrusts the execution of foreign commissions to his collaborators, surveys from afar their serial productions, takes care not to interfere, as if fearful of allowing the tiniest spangle of his talent to venture beyond his native soil—European distribution rights are available for only his B pictures. In the Uffizi, the Prado, the National Gallery, the Louvre, in Munich and in Vienna, we find Raphael, Titian, a hundred others. Every painter, or almost every painter, except Tintoretto. He fiercely guarded his works for his fellow citizens and the only way to find out anything about him is to search for him in his native city for the very good reason that he did not *want* to leave Venice.

But we must be specific. In Venice itself he has two distinct clienteles. He besieges public officials and, naturally, puts his whole studio to work, including the head of the family, if the Senate gives him a commission. Still visible in the Doge's Palace, under a lighting system that shows them off to advantage, are the works of a strong collective personality that bore the name of Tintoretto. But if you are interested in Jacopo Robusti you will have to abandon the Piazzetta, cross the Piazza San Marco, ride a donkey across bridges that span the canals, turn down a labyrinth of dark, narrow streets, enter still darker churches. There you will find him. At the Scuola San Rocco you will find him in person, without Marietta or Domenico or Sebastiano Casser; there he works alone. A grimy haze darkens the canvases, or perhaps the lighting is at fault; wait patiently until your eyes become adjusted; finally you will see a rose in the darkness, a genius in the penumbra. And who paid for these paintings? Sometimes the faithful of the parish, sometimes the members of the Brotherhood — middle-class men, great and small; they are his true public, the only public that he loves.

This huckster-painter has none of the qualities of a God-hero. With a little luck he will become notorious, famous, but never glorious; his profane clientele lacks the power to crown him. Of course the renown of his august colleagues honors the whole profession and he, too, scintillates somewhat. Does he covet their glory? Perhaps. But he meets none of the requirements for acquiring glory; he rejects the favor of princes because it would reduce him to servitude. Jacopo Robusti takes pride in remaining a petty chief, a peddler of Fine Arts made to order, the master of his own studio. He makes no difference between the economic independence of the producer and the freedom of the artist; his activities prove that he has a secret desire to reverse the laws of marketing, to create demand by supplying goods. Did he not create slowly and patiently within the Brotherhood of San Rocco a demand for art — a certain kind of art — which he alone could satisfy? His independence is preserved to an even greater degree when he works for associations — *consorterie*, parishes — and when these great bodies make their decisions by majority vote.

Michelangelo, a pseudo-noble, and Titian, the son of peasants, are directly exposed to the attraction of the monarchy. Tintoretto's heritage is that of the independent craftsman and worker. The artisan is an amphibian; as a manual worker, he is proud of his hands, and as a member of the petty bourgeoisie, he is attracted by the ruling bourgeoisie. By fostering competition the ruling bourgeoisie allows fresh air to circulate within a stifling protectionism. At that time there is in Venice *a bourgeois hope*. Only a glimmer, for the aristocracy has long since taken precautions; in their stratified world, rich men are *made*, patricians are born. But restrictions are placed on the wealthy; not only are businessmen and industrialists restricted to their own class but they are also denied entrance into the most lucrative professions; the State restricts the concession of the *appalto* (shipping franchise) to the aristocracy. Sad, dreamy bourgeoisie! Everywhere else in Europe members of the bourgeoisie are hastening to disown their past and buy titles and castles. In Venice everything is denied them, even the humble blessing of betrayal. Betrayal will therefore take the form of dreams. Giovita Fontana, originally from Piacenza, moves into the business world, accumulates gold and spends it in building a palace on the Canale Grande; an entire existence is summed up in these brief words: a voracious desire, satiated, is finally turned into dreamy snobbery, a merchant dies and is reborn as an imaginary patrician. Rich commoners dance in a ring and hide their nocturnal fantasies; grouped into associations they outdo themselves in charitable works, their melancholy austerity contrasting sharply with the melancholy orgies of a disenchanted patriciate.

For the Republic is no longer mistress of the seas. Gradually the aristocracy begins to decline, failures multiply, the number of poor noblemen increases, the others lose their spirit of enterprise. The sons of the merchant princes buy land and live on their income. Soon ordinary "citizens" replace them in certain functions; ships eventually come under the control of men from the bourgeoisie. But the bourgeoisie is still not ready by any stretch of the imagination to consider itself the rising class. It even harbors the notion that it may one day insure the resurgence of the fallen nobility; we should say rather that an obscure agitation took hold of it, making its condition less tolerable and resignation to it more difficult.

Tintoretto does not dream. Never. If ambition is dependent on opportunities for social advancement, then the most ambitious commoners in Venice are the members of the petty bourgeoisie, for they still have the opportunity to rise above their class. But the painter is aware of his deep-seated affinities with his clients. He appreciates their attitude toward work and morality, their good common sense. He likes their nostalgia and, especially, he shares their profound desire for freedom; all of them need freedom, if only to produce and to buy and sell. These are the clues to his opportunism; his is a need for air which comes from the summits. A troubled sky, a distant, invisible ascent opens to him a vertical future; like a balloon he is borne aloft, filled with the new spirit, for since childhood his outlook has been that of the bourgeoisie. But the contradictions within the class of his origin are to limit his ambitions: as a peddler, he hopes always to outdo himself; as a laborer he pretends to work with his hands. That is enough to determine his position. There are in Venice approximately 7,600 patricians, 13,600 citizens, 127,000 artisans, workers and small businessmen, 1,500 Jews, 12,900 domestics and 550 beggars. Ignoring the Jews and nobles, beggars and domestics, Tintoretto is interested only in the imaginary barrier that separates the commoners into two groups, 13,600 on the one hand and 127,000 on the other. He wants to be first in the second group and last in the first — in short, the most humble of the rich and the most distinguished of the tradesmen. This makes the artisan, in the heart of troubled Venice, a pseudo-bourgeois more true than a true bourgeois. In him and on his canvases the Brotherhood of San Rocco will admire the embellished image of a bourgeoisie untainted by betrayal.

Michelangelo has reservations about working for the Sovereign Pontiff; his contempt sometimes makes him recoil, for this nobleman looks down on art. Tintoretto is just the opposite; he outstrips himself; without art, what would he be? A dyer. Art is the

28

force that lifts him above his natal condition, and his dignity is the thing that sustains him. He has to work or to fall back to the bottom of the well. Recoil from art? Keep away from it? How? He has no time to raise questions about painting. Who knows whether he even gives it a second thought? Michelangelo thinks too much; he is a gentleman, an intellectual. Tintoretto does not meditate — he paints.

So much for his opportunism. His destiny is to incarnate bourgeois puritanism in an aristocratic Republic during its decline. Elsewhere this somber humanism would take root; in Venice it will disappear before being recognized for what it is, but not before arousing the distrust of an aristocracy always on guard. The moroseness that official and bureaucratic Venice manifests toward Tintoretto is the same as that which the patriciate evidences toward the Venetian bourgeoisie. These cantankerous merchants and their painter pose a danger to the Establishment and have to be kept under surveillance.

MAN AT BAY

There is something superb about Tintoretto's stubborn refusal to compete: "I acknowledge no rival and accept no judge." Michelangelo would probably say that. The bad part is that Tintoretto does not. Quite the opposite: when invited to present a sketch, he will lose no time in accepting. Afterwards, we know that he releases his bolts of lightning. Yes, somewhat in the same manner that a cuttle-fish scatters its ink. Blinded by lightning, spectators are unable to see his picture clearly. Everything is arranged, moreover, so that they need never study it or — more important still — appreciate it. When they come out of their stupor, the canvas is in place, the offer under seal, and they will have seen only the flash. Either I am badly mistaken or he is being evasive; he seems to be afraid to come face to face with his adversaries. Would he waste all this ingenuity if he felt certain that his talent would suffice? Would he deign to astound his contemporaries through the quantity of his output if they had no reservations about its quality?

And then rivalry brings to the fore his mania for self-affirmation through self-effacement; this is his strong point, his trademark. The slightest criticism upsets him, offends him. In 1559 the San Rocco church commissioned the *Healing of the Paralytic* to balance a canvas by Pordenone. No one asks him to imitate the style of his predecessor. There is no cause for rivalry,[1] for Antonio di Sacchis has been dead for twenty years; and if it was once possible for him to influence the younger painter, that time has passed, for Jacopo has mastered his art. Still, he is unable to resist the temptation; he has to paint in the style of Pordenone. Attention

1. Ridolfi, deceived by the resemblance of their styles, declared that the canvas was painted "in concurrenza con il Pordenone."

30

has been focused on the way in which he "exaggerates the baroque violence of their gestures . . . by contrasting his monumental figures with the architecture inside which they are compressed" and "achieved this effect by lowering the ceiling . . . and using the columns themselves . . . to immobilize the gestures, freeze their violence." He shudders at the notion of being forever imprisoned in an inert confrontation: "Compare, if you like, one Pordenone with the other; I, Jacopo Robusti, am leaving." He has, of course, taken pains to have the spurious Di Sacchis outshine the real Di Sacchis. His retreat is not a rout; he issues a parting challenge: "Old or young, I take them all on and beat them on their own ground." But this is precisely the thing that arouses suspicion. Why would he need to play their game and submit to their rules if he could outshine them all by being himself? What resentment in his insolence! This Cain assassinates every Abel preferred over him: "You like this Veronese? Well, I can do much better when I deign to imitate him; you take him for a man and he is nothing but a technique." And what humility. From time to time this pariah slips into the skin of another person in order to enjoy in his turn the delight of being loved. And then at times it would seem that he lacks the courage to manifest his scandalous genius; disheartened, he leaves his genius in semidarkness and tries to prove it *deductively*: "Since I paint the best Veroneses and the best Pordenones, just imagine *what I am capable of painting* when I allow myself to be me." As a matter of fact, he almost never takes the liberty of being himself unless someone builds up his confidence and leaves him alone in an empty room. This lack of self-confidence has its origin, of course, in the hostility manifested toward him by others. But the painter's timidity and his fellow citizens' bias have their source in the same disease; in 1548, in Venice, under Tintoretto's attack against patricians, connoisseurs and aesthetes, *painting is in jeopardy*.

* * *

A long evolution has begun — an evolution which will substitute everywhere the profane for the sacred. Cold, glittering, rimy, the diverse branches of human activity emerge one after the other from mellow divine promiscuity. Art has its turn, and from the settling mists emerges a sumptuous disenchantment, painting. It still recalls the time when Duccio and Giotto were showing God his Creation just as it had left his hands, after he had recognized it as his work, put the world in its frame for all eternity, and closed the books of the whole affair. Into the picture, the fief of the Sun and the supreme Eye, monks and prelates sometimes slipped their transparency; they came tiptoeing in to view what God was viewing, then excused themselves and went away. Finished: the Eye is closed, Heaven blind. What is the result? First a change of clientele. As long as the work was done for the clergy, all went well; but the day the biggest of the Florentine bankers had the ridiculous notion of using frescos to beautify his house, The Omnipotent One, dismayed, began to buttress his claim to the role of Lover of Souls. Then, too, there was the Florentine affair, the conquest of perspective. Perspective is profane; sometimes even, it is a profanation. Observe Mantegna's Christ lying feet first and head remote; do you think that the Father is satisfied with a foreshortened Son?* God is absolute proximity, universal envelopment by love; can He be shown *from a distance* the Universe that He has created and that He is at each instant saving from annihilation? Is Being to conceive and produce Non-Being? The Absolute to engender the Relative? Light to contemplate Shadow? Reality to be taken for Appearance? No, this would be a renewal of the eternal story: Ingenuity, the Tree of Knowledge, Original Sin and Expulsion. This time the Apple is called perspective. But the Florentine Adamites nibble at it rather than eat it, thereby avoiding immediate discovery of their Fall. During the middle of the Quattrocento, Uccello thinks that he is still in Paradise, and poor Alberti, the

*Andrea Mantegna (1431-1506) began at an early age to experiment with traditional subjects. His most daring achievement is the unorthodox image of Christ in the ungainly position from which medical students might have viewed his deathly pallor and open wounds.

theoretician of the "perspectivists," is still trying to present geometrical optics as an Ontology of Visibility; he is rather ingenuous in asking the Divine Look to guarantee convergent lines. Heaven has failed to heed this absurd request, relegating man to the nothingness which is properly his and which he has just rediscovered once again; distance, isolation, separation — these negations set our bounds; only man has a horizon. Alberti's window opens on a measurable universe, but this rigid miniature depends wholly on the point that defines both concentration and dispersion — the eye. In Piero della Fra Francesca's Annunciation, between the Angel and the Virgin we see retreating columns; this is an illusion, for in themselves and for their Creator none of these inert white columns, identical and incomparable, have ever stirred in their sleep. Perspective is an act of violence which human weakness is forcing upon God's little world. A hundred years later in the Netherlands Being will be rediscovered at the very heart of appearing and appearance will reclaim the dignity of apparition; painting will have new aims and will acquire new meaning. But before Vermeer can give us the sky, the stars, day and night, the moon and the earth in the form of a tiny brick wall, the bourgeoisie from the North must win their greatest victories and forge their humanism.

In sixteenth-century Italy faith still burns in the artists' hearts, combatting the atheism of their hands and eyes. In their attempt to get a firmer grasp on the Absolute, they perfect techniques which force upon them a Relativism which they detest. These mystified dogmatists can neither push forward nor retrace their steps. If God no longer looks at the images that they paint, who will replace Him? Their images are but the reflection of man's impotence; what will validate them? If the sole aim of painting is to gauge our myopia, it is not worth one hour's labor. To reveal man to the Omnipotent One who deigned to raise him from the clay was an act of thanksgiving, a sacrifice. But why reveal man to man? Why reveal him *as he is not?* The artists born near the end of the century, around 1480 — Titian, Giorgione, Raphael — pay lip service to heaven. More about this later. And then the wealth and efficacy of means still disguise the sinister indetermination of ends. Furthermore, we can surmise that Raphael had a presentiment of those ends; he mocked everyone and everything, caroused with women, sold chromos, and through his *Schadenfreude* incited his collaborators to produce obscene engravings. Insincerity means suicide. At any rate the serenity of painting vanishes with these sacred monsters. In the second quarter of the century painting runs amuck as a result of its own perfection. In the barbaric taste which contemporaries evidenced for great "realizations," a certain uneasiness is manifested; the public demands that the painter utilize all the pomp of realism to conceal his subjectivity, that he efface himself before life, blot out all memory of himself; ideally it should be as if one came upon the pictures by surprise, somewhere in the forest, and saw persons springing from the canvas and splinters from the broken frame flying at the throats of passers-by. The object should reabsorb its visibility, contain it, turn attention away from it by continuously appealing to all the senses, and particularly to the sense of touch; every artifice should be employed to replace the *representation* by a hollow participation of the spectator in the spectacle, so that horror and tenderness would thrust men against their images and, if possible, into their midst, so that desire, burning all the fires of perspective, would discover the *ersatz* of divine ubiquity — the immediate presence of flesh; the logic of the heart. What is desired is *the thing itself* and its destruction: bigger than nature, more real, more beautiful — Terror. But Terror is a disease of rhetoric. Art will slink away, ashamed, once it has lost its letters of credit. Fettered, kept under surveillance, subjected to restrictions imposed by the State, the Church and taste, more sought after and honored, perhaps, than ever before, the artist for the first time in history becomes conscious of his solitude. Who gave him this mandate? What is the source of the right which he arrogates to himself? God has gone out, Darkness reigns. How can he paint in the dark? And *whom?* And *what?* And *why?* The object of art is still the world, that Absolute, but *Reality* steals away, reversing the relation between the finite and the infinite. A vast plenitude has been supporting the wretchedness of bodies and their fragility; now fragility becomes the sole plenitude, the unique surety. The Infinite is emptiness, darkness, inside and outside the creature; the Absolute is absence, it is God sequestered in human souls, it is desertion. It is too late to *portray,* too early to *create;* the painter is in hell; something comes to birth: a new damnation — genius, that uncertainty, that foolish desire to traverse the world's darkness and contemplate it from without, to crush it against walls and canvases, to sift out its unknown splendors. Genius — a new word in Europe, a conflict between the Relative and the Absolute, between a finite presence and an infinite absence. For the painter knows full well that he will not leave the world, that even if he could, he would bear with him everywhere the Nothingness that transpierces him; he can not transcend perspective without first acquiring the right to create other plastic spaces.

Michelangelo dies obsessed, summing up his despair and scorn in these two words: original sin. Tintoretto says nothing; he practices deceit, for if he acknowledged his solitude, he would find it unbearable. But for that very reason we can understand that he suffers from it more than anyone else; our spurious bourgeois, working for the bourgeoisie, lacks even the alibi of glory. In the pit of vipers the little dyer thrashes about, infected with the moral neurosis which Henri Jeanson so aptly named "the frightening moral robustness of the ambitious"; he sets modest objectives for himself: to rise above his father through the judicious exploitation of his talents, to corner the market by flattering public taste. Lighthearted opportunism, cunning, speed, talent — nothing is lacking and everything is undermined by a vertiginous void, by Art without God. This Art is ugly, mean, dark; it is the imbecile passion of the part for the whole, an icy, tenebrous wind blowing through perforated hearts. Drawn by the void, Jacopo sets out on a motionless voyage from which he will never return.

Genius does not exist; it is the scandalous audacity of Nothingness. He, the Little Dyer, exists and knows his limitations; this level-headed boy wants simply to mend the rent. All he asks is a modest plenitude; how can Infinity concern him? And how is

35

he to know that one stroke of his brush is enough to confound his judges? His mean, stubborn ambition will be unleashed in the Darkness of Ignorance. After all, it is not his fault if painting is a lost dog with no collar; later there will be fools who will rejoice over their Abandonment; in mid-sixteenth century Italy, the first victim of monocular perspective seeks to hide his. To work alone and for nothing is to die of fear. One must have arbiters. At any price. God has died away, Venice remains — Venice which can fill up holes, seal cavities, plug outlets, stop hemorrhages and leaks. In the Doge's Republic good subjects have to consider the State in all their activities; painters must paint to beautify the city. Jacopo places himself at the disposal of his fellow citizens; they formulate a certain academic notion of Art which he is quick to adopt. All the more so since he has always had the same notion; it was explained to him when he was a small child, and he believed it: an artisan's worth is measured by the number and importance of the commissions that he receives, the honors that he is accorded. He will hide his genius under his opportunism and consider social success the sole obvious sign of a mystical victory. His deception blinds others; on the earth he plays poker and cheats; and then he gambles on heaven, without deception. If he wins down here with all the aces that he pulls from his sleeve, he dares to pretend that he will win up there; if he sells his canvases, this means that he has snared the world. But who could blame him for his malice? It is the nineteenth century that pronounced the divorce of the artist and the public; in the sixteenth, it is *true* that painting is running amuck; it has ceased to be a religious sacrifice; but it is *equally true* that it is being rationalized — it is becoming a social service. Who then would dare to say, in Venice: "I paint for myself, serve as my own witness"? And as for those who say this today, are we sure that they are telling the truth? Everyone is a judge, no one is; make what you will of that. Tintoretto is more to be pitied than blamed; his Art cuts through his age like a flaming sword, but he can see it only through the eyes of his time. Besides, he has chosen his own hell; thereupon the Finite again closes up over the Infinite, ambition over genius, Venice over her painter who will never again emerge. But captive Infinity gnaws away at everything; Jacopo's calculated opportunism turns to a frenzy; now he has not only to succeed but also to *prove*. A voluntary culprit, the unfortunate painter has made himself party to an endless trial; acting as his own attorney, he has made each painting a witness for the defense and has never ceased to plead his case. There is a city to convince, with its magistrates and its bourgeoisie whose verdict, to be rendered solely by them and not subject to appeal, will determine his mortal future and his immortality. He and he alone is responsible for the strange amalgam; he has to choose between drawing up a code for his own court of last resort and transforming the Republic of Venice into a supreme tribunal. He makes the only choice possible under the circumstances. Unfortunately for him. How well I understand his indifference toward the rest of the universe! He is not concerned with the opinion of the Germans or even the Florentines. Venice is the most beautiful, the richest; she has the best painters, the best critics, the most enlightened patrons of art. *Here*, inside the brick walls, between a tiny patch of sky and still water, under the flamboyant absence of the Sun, Eternity will be won, lost, in a single lifetime, forever.

Well and good. But why cheat? Why deck himself out in the trappings of Veronese? If he wants his genius to arouse admiration, why does he smother it so frequently? And why does he name judges only to corrupt them and deceive them?

Why? Because the court is prejudiced, his cause lost, his sentence set, and he knows it. In 1548 he asks Venice to bear witness to the Infinite; she becomes frightened and refuses. What a destiny! Abandoned by God, he has to practice deceit in choosing judges; having found them, he has to cheat in order to have his case adjourned. Throughout his life he will keep them in suspense, sometimes fleeing, sometimes turning on them and blinding them. Everything has its place: suffering and ill-humor, arrogance, flexibility, tremendous effort, rancor, implacable pride and the humble desire to be loved. Tintoretto's painting is first and foremost a passionate love affair between a man and a city.

37

A MOLE IN THE SUN

In this senseless romance the city is apparently even more foolish than the man. She has not failed to honor all her other painters. Then why evidence toward this one, the greatest of them all, sullen distrust, moroseness? For the simple reason that she is in love with someone else.

The Republic of Venice is hungry for prestige. Her ships have long accounted for her glory; tired and threatened with decline, she flaunts an artist. Titian alone is worth a fleet. From tiaras and crowns he has stolen flakes of fire to fashion for himself a halo. His adopted land admires him *first and foremost* because of the respect that he inspires in the Emperor; in the sacred light, awesome but perfectly harmless, which encircles his cranium, Venice pretends to recognize her own glory. The painter of kings can be nothing less than the king of painters; the Queen of the Seas acknowledges him as her son and through him recovers a trace of majesty. She has at once given him a profession, a reputation; but when he works for kings, he is suffused with divine light which seeps through walls and spreads as far as San Marco; then she knows that he is repaying a hundredfold what he has received from her. He is a National Asset. Furthermore, this man has the longevity of trees; he endures for a century and unobtrusively becomes an Institution. The presence of an academy consisting of one member born before them and determined to survive them is demoralizing to young artists; it exasperates them and stunts their ambitions. They imagine that their city has the power to immortalize the living and that Venice has reserved this favor for Titian alone. A victim of this misunderstanding, Tintoretto — under the fallacious pretext "I am entitled to it" — demands the same recognition as his illustrious predecessor. But worth is not subject to litigation; one cannot demand from a Republic some-

38

thing which belongs by right to a hereditary monarchy. Jacopo is wrong in upbraiding the Doge's City for focusing all reflectors toward the baobab of the Rialto; the reverse is true. A pencil of light whose source is Rome or Madrid—outside the walls, at any rate —strikes the ancient trunk and reflects onto Venice, eliminating the shadows through a sort of indirect lighting. And I, too, was about to make a mistake, for I first thought of entitling this chapter "In Titian's Shadow." The truth is that *Titian cast no shadow.* Weigh this carefully: on the day of Jacopo's birth the old man is forty; he is seventy-two when his young rival first tries to assert himself. That would be the moment for him to step down, to fade away gracefully. Nothing doing! The indomitable monarch reigns on for twenty-seven years. When he finally disappears, the centenarian has the supreme good fortune of leaving an unfinished *Pietà*—like a youthful dream cut short. For more than half a century Tintoretto the Mole burrows in a labyrinth whose walls are splattered with glory; until the age of fifty-eight the nocturnal beast is hemmed in by sunlight, blinded by the implacable celebrity of an Other. When the light is finally extinguished, Jacopo Robusti is old enough to die but insists on surviving the tyrant. He will gain nothing thereby, however, for Titian is adroit enough to combine two contradictory functions and to serve as an employee of the Court without relinquishing his independence as a petty employer—a happy circumstance not often found in history, and certainly not in the case of Tintoretto, who has put all his eggs in one basket. Visit both tombs and you will see the price he is still paying for his sacrifice to his country. The radioactive corpse of the Grand Old Man lies buried under a mountain of embellishments at Santa Maria dei Frari, a veritable cemetery of Doges; Tintoretto's corpse rests beneath a slab in the murky darkness of a parish church. To me, this is well and good. Titian has the garnish, the sugar and spice, and this is poetic justice; I even wish that he had been buried in Rome beneath Victor Emmanuel's monument, the most hideous in all Italy except for Milan's Grand Central Station. Against this, Jacopo has the horror of naked stone; his name is sufficient. But since this is strictly a personal opinion, I can understand why an irritated traveler would ask Venice for an explanation: "Ungrateful town, is that the best you could do for the best of your sons? Mean city, why do you put floodlights around Titian's *Assumption* and stint on electricity for Robusti's canvases?" I know the explanation; it appeared in 1599 in Aretino's correspondence: "If Robusti wants to be honored, why doesn't he paint like Vecellio?" Jacopo will hear the same refrain every day of his life; it will be repeated before his canvases after his death as well as before, and it is still heard today: "Why does he paint like this? Why does he stray from the Royal Way prepared for him? Our great Vecellio has carried painting to such heights of perfection that no further progress is possible; newcomers will have to follow in the Master's footsteps or Art will fall back into barbarism." Fickle Venetians! Inconsequential bourgeois! Tintoretto is *their* painter; he portrays what they see and feel; this they can not endure. Titian ridicules them, and they worship him.* Titian spends most of his time soothing princes, reassuring them through his canvases that everything is for the best in this best of all possible worlds. Discord is but an illusion, archenemies are secretly reconciled by the colors of their cloaks. Violence? only a ballet danced half-heartedly by spurious he-men with downy beards. Such is his method of depreciating wars. The painter's art borders on the apologetic, becomes a theodicy: suffering, injustice, evil do not exist; nor does mortal sin; Adam and Eve sinned only in order that they might have the opportunity to know and to make known to us that they were naked. In a magnificent quadruple gesture God, noble and benevolent, leaning out from his Heaven, stretches out His arms toward the upraised arms of supine Man. Order reigns; quelled and enslaved, perspective respects hierarchies; discreet accommodations assure kings and saints of preferred positions. If someone is lost in the distance, shrouded by the haze that envelops vague terrain or obscured by smoke from remote lamps, this is never by accident. The in-

*Titian Tiziano Vecellio (c. 1477-1576) owed his enormous success as a portraitist to his ability to paint each subject's ideal of himself.

40

distinctness of the figure corresponds to the obscurity of his condition; besides, it helps to focus attention on the patches of light in the foreground. The artist pretends with his brush to relate an event or record a ceremony; by sacrificing movement to order and contrast to unity, he makes his brush caress bodies rather than copy them. Not one of the bearded persons witnessing the Assumption is individualized. First come several legs and upraised arms — a flaming bush; then the substance is impregnated with an element of differentiation and engenders fleeting figures scarcely distinguishable from the collective background which can at any moment reabsorb them — such is the condition of the underlings; Titian reserves individuality for the Great. Even here, however, he is careful to round off their angles; sharp lines isolate, create distance, signify pessimism; the courtesan, who is a professional optimist, directs a symphony of colors proclaiming God's glory, which he epitomizes and mitigates. Titian then applies the finishing touches; he scrapes and polishes, applies lacquers and varnishes. Sparing no effort to hide his labor, he manages finally to remove every trace of himself from the canvas. The stroller enters an unobstructed area, walks among flowers under a proper sun; the proprietor is dead; the stroller is so lonely that he forgets himself and disappears. The result is treason of the worst sort: the betrayal of Beauty.

For once the traitor has the excuse of believing in what he is doing. He is not a townsman but a transplanted peasant; when he arrives in Venice, he comes as a rustic child of the middle ages. The country youth has long nurtured a popular, reverent love for the nobility; he makes his way through the bourgeoisie without even seeing it and rejoins his true masters at the summit, all the more certain of pleasing them because they have his sincere respect. We frequently hear that he secretly considered himself their equal; this, I think, is completely false. What would have been the source of his light? He is a vassal; raised to the peerage through the glory that only kings can dispense, he owes to them everything, even his pride; why would he choose to turn against them? He looks upon his haughty serenity, the hierarchy of power and the beauty of the world as complementary reflexes; in the best possible faith he puts the bourgeois techniques of the Renaissance to the service of feudalism — he has stolen their tool.

Yet he is admired by both the bourgeoisie and the patriciate. He provides the Venetian technocrats with an alibi by speaking of happiness, glory and preordained harmony at the time they are making laudable efforts to obscure their decline. Every merchant, whether a nobleman or a commoner, is captivated by the sanctimonious canvases that reflect the tranquility of kings. If all is for the best, if evil is but a beautiful illusion, if each keeps forever his hereditary place in the divine and social hierarchy, then this means that nothing has happened for the last hundred years: the Turks have not taken Constantinople, Columbus has not discovered America, the Portuguese have not even dreamed of dumping spices or the continental powers of forming a coalition against the Republic of Venice. People had thought that the Barbary pirates were threatening the seas, that the African source of precious metals had been exhausted, that the scarcity of money had slowed down transactions during the first half of the century and that then suddenly an outpouring of Peruvian gold from the Spanish waterworks had reversed the tide, raised prices, flooded the market — but that was only a dream. Venice still reigns over the Mediterranean; she is at the pinnacle of her power, wealth and grandeur. In other words, they want Beauty, these uneasy souls, because it is reassuring. I understand them, for I have boarded a plane two hundred times without ever becoming reconciled to it. I am too earth-bound to consider flying normal; occasionally fear surges up — especially when my companions are as ugly as I; but if there is on board a beautiful woman or a handsome boy or a charming couple in love, my fear vanishes; ugliness is a prophecy — it trails a certain element of extremism which seeks to carry negation to the point of horror. Beauty seems indestructible; its sacred image protects us; so long as we have it in our presence, no catastrophe will occur. The same is true of Venice; she is beginning to fear that she will sink into the mire of her lagoons; imagining that she will find salvation through

Beauty, the supreme levity, she makes a pretense of transforming her palaces and canvases into buoys and floats. Those responsible for Titian's success are the very ones who desert the sea, who try to escape their disenchantment through orgies, who prefer the security of ground rent to profit from commerce.

Tintoretto is born in a troubled town; he breathes Venetian uneasiness, is consumed by Venetian uneasiness, can paint nothing but Venetian uneasiness. If they were in his place, his severest critics would behave no differently. But they are not; they can not escape uneasiness but wish not to have it brought to their attention; they condemn paintings that *represent* it. Fate has decreed that Jacopo unwittingly expose an age which refuses to recognize itself. Now we understand the meaning of his destiny and the secret of Venetian malice. Tintoretto displeases everyone: patricians because he reveals to them the puritanism and fanciful agitation of the bourgeoisie; artisans because he destroys the corporate order and reveals, under their apparent professional solidarity, the rumblings of hate and rivalry; patriots because the frenzied state of painting and the absence of God discloses to them, under his brush, an absurd and unpredictable world in which anything can occur, *even* the death of Venice. It would seem that this painter who has assimilated bourgeois culture might at least find favor with the class that he has adopted. Not so. The bourgeoisie will accept him only with reservations; it always finds him fascinating, but often it finds him terrifying. The reason is that it has not recognized itself for what it is. Signor de Zigninoni must have dreamed of betrayal; he was searching covertly for a means of acceding to the patriciate, of escaping from the bourgeois reality that he was helping in spite of himself to create. What he finds most distasteful in Robusti's paintings is their radicalism and their "demystifying" virtues. In short, it is necessary at any price to refute Tintoretto's testimony, to make it seem that he has failed in his venture, to deny the originality of his research, *to get rid of him.*

Consider the charges brought against him: *first,* that he works too fast and leaves his imprint everywhere. People want smooth, finished work, especially *the impersonal element;* if the painter portrays himself, he is subjecting himself to interrogation and thereby putting the public on trial. Venice imposes on her artists the maxim of the puritans: "No personal remarks." She is careful to equate Jacopo's lyricism with the callous haste of a jaded contractor. Then comes Ridolfi's charge that Tintoretto wrote on the walls of his studio: "The color of Titian combined with the drawing of Michelangelo." The charge is baseless; the statement first appears in 1548 in the writings of a Venetian art critic and does not refer to Robusti. The latter, in fact, could have known the works of Michelangelo only through reproductions by Daniele de Volterra — consequently, *not before* 1557. And could anyone take those words at face value? Is it conceivable that he would try *seriously* to follow the absurd formula? The legend is but a dream of his age; confronted by the Spanish menace, the Northern states and the Central states dream of forming an alliance — too late. But the awakening of a national consciousness, though brief, can not fail to have a transient influence on the Fine Arts. "Michelangelo and Titian" means Florence and Venice. How nice for painting to be unified!

Nothing serious, obviously. The dream is inoffensive so long as it is everyone's dream. But those who pretend to see in it the obsession of Robusti *alone* must have wanted to destroy the artist by lodging in the heart of his art an explosive nightmare. Color is Jake laughing; drawing, Jake crying. In the first instance unity, in the second the risk of disorder. On the one hand the harmony of the spheres, on the other abandonment. The two Titans of the century throw themselves on each other, embrace each other, try to stifle each other — Jacopo is the theater of operations. And sometimes Titian wins by a hair and sometimes Michelangelo barely manages to claim the match. In either case, the loser is strong enough to spoil the winner's triumph, and the result of the Pyrrhic victory is a botched picture. Botched through excess. Tintoretto seems to his contemporaries like an insane Titian, devoured by Buonarroti's somber passion, shaken by St. Vitus's dance — possessed, a freakish split-personality. In one sense Jacopo exists only as a battlefield; in another sense he is a monster, a fraud. Vasari's fable becomes crystal clear: Adam Robusti wanted to taste the fruits of the tree of knowledge and Archangel Tiziano, pointing his finger and flapping his wings, chased him out of Paradise. To have bad luck or to bring bad luck is still one and the same in Italy. If you have recently had financial troubles or an automobile accident, if you have broken your leg or lost your wife, do not expect to be invited to dinner; a hostess would not wittingly expose her other guests to premature baldness, a head cold or, in extreme cases, to a broken neck caused by a fall on her stairway. I knew a Milanese who had the evil eye; this was discovered last year; he no longer has a single friend, and he dines alone, at home. Such is Jacopo: a caster of spells because a spell was cast on him. Or perhaps on his mother when she was carrying him. The spell actually has its source in Venice: uneasy, accursed, she has produced a troubled soul and placed a curse on his uneasiness. The unfortunate victim loves a despairing and uncompromising town to the point of despair, and his love horrifies the beloved. When Tintoretto passes by, people step aside: he smells of death. Exactly. But what other odor is given off by patrician festivities and bourgeois charity and the docility of the people? Pink houses with flooded cellars and walls crisscrossed by rats? What odor is given off by stagnant canals with their urinous cresses and by grey mussels fastened with squalid cement to the underside of quays? In the depths of a river a bubble is clinging to the mud; broken loose by the eddies formed by gondolas, it rises through murky water, breaks through the surface, spins around, glistens and bursts; everything crumbles away when the blister bursts — bourgeois nostalgia, the grandeur of the Republic, God and Italian painting.

Tintoretto was the chief mourner for Venice and a way of life, but when he died there was no one to act as his chief mourner; then silence fell, and hypocritically pious hands hung crepe over his canvases. When we remove this black veil, we find a portrait, started anew a hundred times. The portrait of Jacopo? The portrait of the Queen of the Seas? As you will: the city and her painter have one and the same face.

45

THE PAINTINGS OF GIACOMETTI*

From the back of the room where I was sitting at the Sphinx, I could see several nude women. The distance that separated us (the glossy wood floor seemed insuperable even though I wanted to walk across it) impressed me as much as did the women.[1]

The result: four inaccessible figurines balanced on the edge of a vertical background formed by the floor. Giacometti painted them as he saw them — *from a distance*. Still, the four women have an arresting presence. They seem to be poised on the floor, ready at any moment to drop down upon him like the lid on a box.

I have often seen them, especially in the evening, in a little place on the Rue de l'Echaudé, very close and menacing.

Distance, far from being an accident, is in his eyes part and parcel of every object. These whores, twenty steps away — twenty impossible steps away — are forever outlined in the light of his hopeless desire. His studio is an archipelago, a conglomeration of

---

*Originally published in *Les Temps Modernes* (June, 1954). Alberto Giacometti (1901-   ) belongs to an artistic Swiss family. Unchanged by success, he has worked since 1927 in a two-room studio in the industrial section of Paris. His paintings are for the most part studies of himself, his wife Annette and his brother Diego. His best known sculptures are probably *Three Men Walking* (1949), *Walking Quickly Under the Rain* (1949), and *Man Crossing a Square on a Sunny Morning* (1950). Known primarily as a surrealist in the early 1930's, he went through a long period of experimentation and emerged in the 1940's as one of the world's most controversial sculptors. Defining art as "an absurd activity," he has evolved elongated figures expressing nihilism and despair, terror and doom.

1. Letter to Matisse (November, 1950).

irregular distances. The Mother Goddess against the wall retains all the nearness of an obsession. When I retreat, she advances; when I am farthest away, she is closest. The small statue at my feet is a man seen in the rear-view mirror of an automobile — in the act of disappearing; moving closer to the statue is to no avail, for the distance cannot be traversed. These solitudes repel the visitor with all the insuperable length of a room, a lawn, or a glade that none would dare to cross. They stand as proof of the paralysis that grips Giacometti at the sight of his equal.

It does not follow, however, that he is a misanthropist. His aloofness is mixed with fear, often with admiration, sometimes with respect. He is distant, of course, but man creates distance while distance has no meaning outside human space. Distance separates Hero from Leander and Marathon from Athens but not one pebble from another.

I first understood what distance is one evening in April, 1941. I had spent two months in a prison camp, which was like being in a can of sardines, and had experienced absolute proximity; the boundary of my living space was my skin; night and day I felt against my body the warmth of a shoulder or a bosom. This was not incommodious, for the others were *me*.

That first evening, a stranger in my home town, having not yet found my old friends, I opened the door of a café. Suddenly I was frightened — or almost; I could not understand how these squat, corpulent buildings could conceal such deserts. I was lost; the scattered patrons seemed to me more distant than the stars. Each of them could claim a vast seating area, a whole marble table while I, to touch them, would have had to cross over the "glossy floor" that separated us.

If they seemed inaccessible to me, these men who were scintillating comfortably in their bulbs of rarefied gas, it was because I no longer had the right to place my hand on their shoulders and thighs or to call one of them "knuckle-head." I had re-entered middle-class society and would have to learn once again to live "at a respectable distance." My attack of agoraphobia had be-

47

trayed my vague feeling of regret for the collective life from which I had been forever severed.

The same applies to Giacometti. For him distance is not a voluntary isolation, nor even a withdrawal. It is something required by circumstances, a ceremony, a recognition of difficulties. It is the product — as he himself said[1] — of forces of attraction and forces of repulsion. He cannot walk a few steps across the glossy floor that separates him from the nude women because he is nailed to his chair by timidity or by poverty; and he feels at this point that the distance is insuperable because he wants to touch their lush flesh. He rejects promiscuity, the fruit of close proximity, because he wants friendship, love. He dares not take for fear of being taken.

His figurines are solitary, but when placed together, no matter how, they are united by their solitude and transformed into a small magical society:

> On observing the figures which, to clear away the table, had been set at random on the floor, I discovered that they formed two groups which seemed to correspond to what I was looking for. I mounted the two groups on bases without the slightest change. . . .

One of Giacometti's scenes is a crowd. He has sculptured men crossing a public square without seeing each other; they pass, hopelessly alone and yet *together;* they will be forever lost from each other, yet would never lose each other if they had not sought each other. He defined his universe better than I possibly could when he wrote, concerning one of his groups, that it reminded him of

> a part of a forest observed during the course of many years . . . a forest in which trees with barren, slender trunks seemed like people who had stopped in their tracks and were speaking to each other.

What is this circular distance — which only words can bridge — if not negation in the form of a *vacuum?* Ironic, defiant, cere-

1. Letter to Matisse (1950).

monious and tender, Giacometti sees space everywhere. "Not everywhere," you will say, "for some objects are in contact." But Giacometti is sure of nothing, not even that. Week after week he was captivated by the legs of a chair: they were not touching the floor. Between things, between men lie broken bridges; the vacuum infiltrates everything, each creature creates its own vacuum.

Giacometti became a sculptor because of his obsession with emptiness. About one statuette he wrote: "Me, rushing down a street in the rain." Sculptors rarely fashion their own busts. Those who do attempt "self-portraits" study themselves from without, in a looking glass. They are the true prophets of objectivity. But imagine a lyrical sculptor: what he tries to reproduce is his inner feeling, the boundless vacuum that surrounds him, leaving him defenseless and exposing him to the storm. Giacometti is a sculptor because he wears his vacuum as a snail its shell, because he wants to explain all its facets and dimensions. And sometimes he finds compatible the modicum of exile that he carries everywhere — and sometimes he finds it horrifying.

A friend once moved in with him. Pleased at first, Giacometti soon became upset: "I opened my eyes one morning and found his trousers and his jacket *in my space.*" At other times, however, he grazes walls and skirts ramparts; the vacuum all around him portends a catastrophe, untoward events, avalanches. In any case he must bear witness to its presence.

* * *

Can he do this through sculpture? By kneading plaster, he creates a vacuum *from a plenum.* The figure when it leaves his fingers is "ten steps away," and no matter what we do, it remains there. The statue itself determines the distance from which it must be viewed, just as courtly manners determine the distance from which the king must be addressed. The situation engenders the surrounding no man's land. Each of his figures is Giacometti himself producing his little local vacuum. Yet all these slight

49

absences that are as much a part of us as our names, as our shadows, are not enough to make a world. There is also the Void, the universal distance between all things. The street is empty, drinking in the sun; suddenly, in this empty space a human being appears.

Sculpture can create a vacuum *from a plenum*, but can it show the plenum arising from what was previously a vacuum? Giacometti has tried a hundred times to answer this question. His composition *"La Cage"* represents his "desire to abolish the socle and have a *limited* space for creating a head and face." That is the crux of his problem, for a vacuum will forever antedate the beings that inhabit it unless it is first surrounded by walls. The "Cage" is "a room that I have seen. I have even seen curtains behind the woman. . . ." On another occasion he made "a figurine in a box between two boxes which are houses." In short, he builds a frame for his figures, with the result that they remain at a certain distance away from us but live in the closed space imposed on them by their individual distances, in the prefabricated vacuum which they cannot manage to fill and which they endure rather than create.

And what is this framed and populated vacuum if not a painting? Lyrical when he sculptures, Giacometti becomes objective when he paints. He tries to capture the features of Annette or of Diego just as they appear in an empty room or in his deserted studio. I have tried elsewhere to show that he approaches sculpture as a painter since he treats a plaster figurine as if it were a person in a painting.* He confers on his statuettes a fixed, imaginary distance. Inversely, I can say that he approached painting as a sculptor since he would like to have us assume that the imaginary space enclosed by a frame is a *true* void. He would like to have us perceive through thick layers of space the woman that he has just painted in a sitting position; he would like for his canvas to be like still water and for us to see the figures *in* the painting as Rimbaud saw a room in a lake — as a transparency.

*See the last essay in this collection.

50

Sculpturing as others paint, painting as others sculpture, is he a painter? Is he a sculptor? Neither, both. Painter and sculptor because his era does not allow him to be both sculptor and architect; sculptor in order to restore to each his circular solitude and painter in order to replace men and things in the world — that is, in the great universal void — he finds it convenient to model what he had at first hoped to paint.[1] At times, however, he knows that only sculpture (or in other instances only painting) will allow him to "realize his impressions." In any case two activities are inseparable and complementary. They allow him to treat from every aspect the problem of his relations with others, whether distance has its origin in them, in him, or in the universe.

*　*　*

How can one paint a vacuum? Before Giacometti it seems that no one had made the attempt. For five hundred years painters had been filling their canvases to the bursting point, forcing into them the whole universe. Giacometti begins by expelling the world from his canvases. For example, he paints his brother Diego all alone, lost in a hangar, and that is sufficient.

A person must also be separated from everything around him. This is ordinarily achieved by emphasizing his contours. But a line is produced by the intersection of two surfaces, and an empty space cannot pass for a surface. Certainly not for a volume. A line is used to separate the container from the content; a vacuum, however, is not a container.

Is Diego "outlined" against the partition behind him? No, the "foreground-background" relation exists only when surfaces are relatively flat. Unless he leans back against it, the distant partition cannot "serve as a background" for Diego; in short, he is in no way connected with it. Or rather he is only because man and object are in the same painting and must therefore maintain

1. For example, his *Nine Figures* (1950): "I had wanted very much to paint them last spring."

51

appropriate relations (hues, values, proportions) for conferring on the canvas its unity. But these correspondences are at the same time erased by the vacuum that interposes itself between them.

No, Diego is not outlined against the gray background of a wall. He is there, the wall is there, that is all. Nothing encloses him, nothing supports him, nothing contains him; he *appears* all alone within the vast frame of empty space.

With each of his paintings Giacometti takes us back to the moment of creation *ex nihilo*. Each painting restates the old metaphysical question: Why is there something rather than nothing? And yet there is something: this stubborn, unjustifiable, superfluous apparition. The painted person is hallucinatory because presented in the form of an interrogative apparition.

* * *

But how can the artist place a figure on his canvas without confining it? Will it not explode in empty space like a fish from the depths on the surface of the water? Not at all. A line represents arrested flight, a balance between the external and the internal; it fastens itself around the shape adopted by an object under the pressure of outside forces; it is a symbol of inertia, of passivity.

Giacometti does not think of finitude as an arbitrary limitation, however. For him the cohesion of an object, its plenitude and its determination are but one and the same effect of its inner power of affirmation. "Apparitions" affirm and confine themselves while defining themselves. Somewhat as the strange curves studied by mathematicians are both encompassing and encompassed, the object encompasses itself.

One day when he had undertaken to sketch me, Giacometti expressed surprise: "What density," he said, "what lines of force!" And I was even more surprised than he since I believe my features to be weak and ordinary. But the reason is that he saw each feature as a centripetal force. A face is forever changing, like a spiral. Turn around: you will never find a contour — only a plenum. The line is the beginning of negation, the passage from being to non-being. But Giacometti holds that reality is pure positivity, that there *is* being and then suddenly there no longer is any, but that there is no conceivable transition from being to nothingness.

Notice how the multiple lines that he draws are *inside* the form depicted. See how they represent intimate relations between being and itself; the fold in a garment, the wrinkle in a face, the protruding of a muscle, the direction of a movement—all these lines are centripetal. They tend to confine by forcing the eye to follow them and leading it always to the center of the figure. The face seems to be contracting under the influence of an astringent substance, giving the impression that in five minutes it will be the size of your fist, like a shrunken head. Still, demarcation of the body is missing. At times the heavy mass of flesh is demarcated vaguely, slyly by a blurred brown nimbus somewhere under the tangly lines of force—and sometimes it is literally unbounded, the contour of an arm or a hip being lost in a dazzling play of light.

We are shown without warning an abrupt dematerialization. For example, a man is shown crossing his legs; as long as I looked only at his head and bust, I was convinced that he had feet. I even thought that I could see them. If I look at them, however, they disintegrate, disappear in a luminous haze, and I no longer know where the void begins and where the body ends. And do not think that this is the same as one of Masson's attempts to disintegrate objects and give them a semblance of ubiquity by scattering them over the whole canvas. If Giacometti fails to demarcate a shoe, the reason is not that he believes it to be unbounded but that he counts on us to add its bounds. They are actually there, these shoes, heavy and dense. To see them, we need only refrain from viewing them in their entirety.

To understand this procedure we need only examine the sketches that Giacometti sometimes makes for his sculptures. Four women on a socle—fine. But let us examine the drawing. First we see the head and neck sketched in bold strokes, then nothing, then an open curve encircling a fixed point—the belly and navel; we also see the stump of a thigh, then nothing, and then two vertical lines and, further down, two others. That is the whole thing. A whole woman. What did we do? We used our knowledge to re-establish continuity, our eyes to join together these *disjecta membra*. We *saw* shoulders and arms on a white paper; we saw them because we had *recognized* a head and torso.

The members were indeed there, though not represented by lines. In the same way we sometimes apprehend lucid, complete ideas that are not represented by words. The body is a current flowing between its two extremities. We are face to face with the absolute reality, the invisible tension of blank paper. But does not the blankness of the paper also represent empty space? Certainly, for Giacometti rejects both the inertia of matter and the inertia of absolute nothingness. A vacuum is a distended plenum, a plenum and oriented vacuum. Reality fulgurates.

* * *

Have you noticed the superabundance of light strokes that striate his torsos and faces? Diego is not solidly stitched but merely basted, in the language of dressmakers. Or could it be that Giacometti wishes "to write luminously on a dark background"? Almost. The emphasis is no longer on separating a plenum from a vacuum but on painting plenitude itself. And since it is at once unity and diversity, how can it be differentiated unless divided? Dark strokes are dangerous, for they risk effacing being, marring it with fissures. If used to outline an eye or encircle a mouth they may create the impression that there are fistules of empty space at the heart of reality. The white striae are there to serve as unseen guides. They guide the eye, determine its movements, dissolve beneath its gaze. But the real danger lies elsewhere.

We are aware of the success of Arcimboldo — his jumbled vegetables and cluttered fish. Why do we find his artifice so appealing? Is it perhaps because the procedure has long been familiar to us? In their own way, have all painters been Arcimboldos? Have they not fashioned, day after day, face after face, each with a pair of eyes, a nose, two ears and thirty-two teeth? Wherein lies the difference? He takes a round cut of red meat, makes two holes in it, sets in each of them a white marble, carves out a nasal appendage, inserts it like a false nose under the ocular spheres, bores a third hole and provides it with white pebbles. Is he not substituting for the indissoluble unity of a face an assortment of heterogenous objects? Emptiness insinuates itself everywhere: between the eyes and eyelids, between the lips, into the nostrils. A head in its turn becomes an archipelago.

You say that this strange assemblage conforms to reality, that the oculist can remove the eye from its orbit or the dentist extract the teeth? Perhaps. But what is the painter to paint? Whatever is? Whatever we see? And what do we see?

Take the chestnut-tree under my window. Some have depicted it as a huge ball, a trembling unity; others have painted its leaves individually, showing their veins. Do I see a leafy mass or a multitude of leaves? I must say that I see both, but neither in its entirety, with the result that I am constantly shifting from one to the other. Consider the leaves: I fail to see them in their entirety, for just as I am about to apprehend them they vanish. Or the leafy mass: just as I am about to apprehend it, it disintegrates. In short I see a swarming cohesion, a writhing dispersion. Let the painter paint that.

And yet Giacometti wants to paint what he sees just as he sees it. He wants the figures at the heart of their original vacuum on his motionless canvas forever to fluctuate between continuity and the discontinuity. He wants the head to be at once isolated because sovereign and reclaimed by the body to serve as a mere periscope of the belly in the sense that Europe is said to be a peninsula of Asia. The eyes, the nose, the mouth — these he wants to make into the leaves of a leafy mass, isolated from each other and blended all together. He succeeds, and this is his supreme triumph.

How does he succeed? By refusing to be more precise than perception. He is not *vague;* he manages rather to suggest through the lack of precision of perception the absolute precision of being. In themselves or for others with a better view, for angels, his faces conform rigidly to the principle of individuation. A glance reveals that they are precise down to the most minute detail; furthermore, we immediately recognize Diego or Annette. That in itself would be sufficient, if required, to cleanse Giacometti of any taint of subjectivism.

At the same time, however, we cannot look at the canvas without uneasiness. We have an irrepressible urge to call for a flashlight or at least a candle. Is it a haze, the fading light of day, or our tired eyes? Is Diego lowering or raising his eyelids? Is he dozing? Is he dreaming? Is he spying? It happens of course that the same questions are asked at popular exhibitions, in front of portraits so bland that any answer is equally appropriate and none mandatory.

The awkward indetermination of popular painters has nothing in common with the calculated indetermination of Giacometti, which might more appropriately be termed overdetermination. I turn back toward Diego and see him alternately asleep and awake, looking at the sky, gazing at me. Everything is true, everything is obvious; but if I bend my head slightly, altering my viewpoint, this truth vanishes and another replaces it. If after a long struggle I wish to adopt one opinion, my only recourse is to leave as quickly as possible. Even then my opinion will remain fragile and probable.

When I discover a face in the fire, for example, or in an inkblot, or in the design of a curtain, the shape that has abruptly appeared becomes rigid and forces itself upon me. Even though I can see it in no other way than this, I know that others will see it differently. But the face in the fire has no truth while in Giacometti's paintings we are provoked and at the same time bewitched by the fact that *there is* a truth and that we are certain of it. It is there, right under my nose, whether I look for it or not. But my vision blurs, my eyes tire, I give up. Then I begin to understand that Giacometti overpowers us because he has reversed the facts in stating the problem.

A painting by Ingres is also instructive. If I look at the tip of the odalisk's nose, the rest of the face is light and soft, like pinkish butter interrupted by the delicate red of the lips; and if I shift my attention to the lips, they emerge from the shadows, moist and slightly parted, and the nose disappears, devoured by the absence of differentiation in the background. I am not bothered by its disappearance, however, for I am secure in the knowledge that I can always recreate it at will.

The reverse holds true in the case of Giacometti. To make a detail seem clear and reassuring all I need do is refrain from centering my attention on it. My confidence is reinforced by what I see through the corner of my eye. The more I look at Diego's eyes the less they communicate to me; but I notice slightly sunken cheeks, a peculiar smile at the corners of the mouth. If my obsession with truth draws my attention down to his mouth, everything immediately escapes me. What is his mouth like? Hard? Bitter? Ironical? Wide-open? Sealed? Against this, *I know* that his eyes, which are almost beyond my range of vision, are half-closed. And nothing prevents me from continuing to turn, obsessed by the phantom face that is constantly being formed, deformed and re-formed behind me. The remarkable part is its credibility. Hallucinations also make their appearance on the periphery only to disappear when viewed directly. But on the other hand, of course. . . .

*   *   *

These extraordinary figures, so perfectly immaterial that they often become transparent and so totally, so fully real that they can be as positive and unforgettable as a physical blow, are they appearing or disappearing? Both. They seem so diaphanous at times that we do not even dream of questioning their features; we have to pinch ourselves to learn whether they really exist. If we insist on examining them, the whole canvas becomes alive; a somber sea rolls over them, leaving only an oil-splotched surface; and then the waves roll back and we see them glistering under the water, white and naked. But their reappearance is marked by a violent affirmation. They are like muffled shouts rising to the top of a mountain and informing the hearer that somewhere someone is grieving or calling for help.

57

The alternation of appearance and disappearance, of flight and provocation, lends to Giacometti's figures a certain air of coquetry. They remind me of Galatea, who fled from her lover under the willows and desired at the same time that he should see her. Coquettish, yes, and graceful because they are pure action, and sinister because of the emptiness that surrounds them, these creatures of nothingness achieve a plenum of existence by eluding and mystifying us.

Every evening an illusionist has three hundred accomplices: his audience and their second natures. He attaches to his shoulder a wooden arm in a bright red sleeve. His viewers expect him to have two arms in identical sleeves; they see two arms, two sleeves, and are satisfied. Meantime a real arm, clothed in black and invisible, produces a rabbit, a card, an explosive cigarette.

Giacometti's art is similar to that of the illusionist. We are his dupes and his accomplices. Without our avidity, our gullibility, the traditional deceitfulness of the senses and contradictions in perception, he could never make his portraits live. He is inspired not only by what he sees but also, and especially, by what he thinks we will see. His intent is not to offer us an exact image but to produce likenesses which, though they make no pretense at being anything other than what they are, arouse in us feelings and attitudes ordinarily elicited by the presence of real men.

At the Grévin Museum one may feel irritated or frightened by the presence of a wax guardian. Nothing would be easier than to construct elaborate farces by capitalizing on that fact. But Giacometti is not particularly fond of farces. With one exception. A single exception to which he has consecrated his life. He has long understood that artists work in the realm of the imaginary, creating illusions, and he knows that "faked monsters" will never produce in spectators anything other than factitious fears.*

In spite of his knowledge, however, he has not lost hope. One

*Sartre's first philosophical work was a study of the imagination, published in France in 1936. It was subsequently published in English in 1948 under the title *Psychology and Imagination* (New York: Philosophical Library).

day he will show us a portrait of Diego just like all others in appearance. We shall be forewarned and know that it is but a phantom, a vain illusion, a prisoner in its frame. And yet on that day, before the mute canvas we shall feel a shock, a very small shock. The very same shock that we feel on returning late and seeing a stranger walking toward us in the dark.

Then Giacometti will know that through his paintings he has brought to birth a real emotion and that his likenesses, without ever ceasing to be illusory, were invested for a few instants with *true* powers. I hope that he will soon achieve this memorable farce. If he does not succeed, no one can. In any case, no one can surpass him.

THE UNPRIVILEGED PAINTER: LAPOUJADE*

Since Goya killers have not ceased their slaughter nor pacifists their protests. Every five or ten years a painter attempts to revive the horrors of war by modernizing uniforms and weapons.**

Lapoujade's undertaking is different. His aim is not to congeal art by putting it to the service of Genteel Thought but rather to study *internally* the nature and scope of painting. Almost a century ago Art became critical; since then it has flaunted its right to judge painting. Lapoujade has evolved his own style while painting and has finally created presences that are an integral part of each composition and yet transcend them all.

His presences could not be communicated through figurative art.*** The human figure, in particular, disguised men's suffering; it disappeared, and its demise within the very matrix of art gave

*Robert Lapoujade was born at Montauban in 1921. According to the biographical notice printed in the catalog prepared for an exhibition of his non-figurative paintings (Galérie Pierre Domec, Paris, March 10 — April 15, 1961), he is a self-made artist, a practitioner "by necessity" of various trades, and a writer. His works have been widely exhibited in Europe and America. The Museum of Modern Art has acquired two of his canvases. This essay was originally printed in the aforementioned catalog.

**Francisco José de Goya (1746-1828), an indefatigable moralist as well as a great artist, depicted the horrors of war in bold colors in *Dos de Mayo* and repeated the same theme in his most famous etchings, *Disasters of War*.

***Since definitions are not always universally accepted (witness the complaint of those who hold that "abstract" art is highly concrete), I have chosen to use the literal equivalents of the French expressions, figurative and non-figurative, rather than contrasts involving "representational," "objective," and the like.

birth to something else — to tortured victims, razed towns, massacred hordes, ubiquitous tormentors. The painter shows us both victims and victors — in short, the portrait of our century. No longer is the object of his art the individual or the typical. It is the singularity and reality of our age. How did Lapoujade manage through the very limitations imposed by abstract art to achieve what figurative art could not?

Since canvases have won the right to be judged solely according to the laws of painting, the artist can reaffirm the fundamental, inviolable link between creativity and beauty. Whatever its provenance, a canvas will be beautiful, or it will not be; daubing is not painting, nor will it look like anything but daubing. Beauty is not the object of art but its flesh and blood, its being. Everyone has always said this, everyone pretends to know it. It is nevertheless true that in abstract art the fundamental link between creativity and beauty, obscured by an alchemist's dream, by the desire to produce a real absolute, is once again revealed in its pristine purity.

At the same time the cliché, "Art for the sake of Art," is reasserted. But this is sheer nonsense! No one paints to create art or to make it be. The artist simply paints. Lapoujade doesn't paint his canvases in the hope of enlarging by a few square centimeters the domain of beauty; but he draws his motifs, his themes, his obsessions, his objectives from the very essence of his art. After the plastic world has dissolved the figures that constrained it, what claim does it have to continued existence? Every work that we see here has the same provenance. *Hiroshima*, like all the others, was preempted *by art*.

This may come as a shock. Politicians began long ago the practice of making minor demands on the services of the artist. Beribboned turncoats have proven time and again that painting dies whenever it is made to serve alien purposes. In fact, until now painters wishing to call attention to the evil done to some men by others were faced with two unpleasant alternatives: they could betray painting without contributing much to morals or, if their work looked beautiful regardless, they could betray the anger or grief of men for Beauty. Either way, the result was treason.

Good sentiments tend toward formalism. If a feeling of righteous indignation is to be communicated, the public must be able to decipher the message; the anxieties of art must be subordinated to false securities. Because Living Beauty is forever evolving, the artist shuns the perplexities inherent in experimentation and elects instead inanimate Beauty. He adopts the most legible transcription, which is necessarily an ancient, conventionalized style of painting.

Attempts to depict acts of violence, mutilated corpses and living bodies racked, tortured and burned have been sterile. By falling back upon visual conventions, artists have shown us a moving side of reality and have conditioned us to react as we normally would — with horror, anger, and especially with the silent flood of sympathy that makes every man experience the wounds of other men as so many holes in his own flesh. This unbearable spectacle puts the spectator to flight. A painting may evidence ingenious composition, correct proportions and harmony, but everything is wasted if the spectator flees and fails to return. And if he should come back, punctured eyes and infected wounds — everything — would disintegrate and beauty would never again be reconstituted. Total failure.

We can be sure that the painter would be called tactless. People would say that he ought to be more discreet, more delicate if he ever again took up such scabrous subjects. Titian, to cite but one name, was known for his tact. Great men of the world could commission him to paint a massacre according to their instructions and could rest assured that he would produce a procession or a ballet. And the result would be beautiful — naturally. Through this procedure torture is eliminated from the canvas just as its scent is eliminated from a painted rose. Murderers dressed in rich garments and dashing mercenaries are shown surveying the operation; as the crowning stroke a victim's bare foot, healthy and alluring, is revealed while his legs, torso and head remain hidden. Tiziano Vecellio was a traitor, for he forced his brush to paint comforting terrors, painless suffering and living corpses. Through him Beauty betrayed man and consorted with kings. For a self-willed man in a room with windows overlooking a concentration camp to paint a compote is not serious; his sin is one of negligence. The real crime would be in painting the concentration camp as if it were a compote — in the same spirit of research and experimentation.

I know of two exceptions. But the first is only apparent. Uncertain and overwhelmed by revulsion and remorse, the tormented visionary Goya painted his visions instead of war. This misguided man lost all desire to guide the masses and finally transformed the horrors of battles and mass murders into the naked horror of being Goya.

Guernica is different.* Here the most fortunate of artists enjoyed the most unprecedented good fortune, with the result that his canvas combined incompatible qualities. Effortlessly. Unforgettable revulsion, commemoration of a massacre, the painting seems nevertheless to have resulted solely from the quest for Beauty; furthermore, the quest was successful. It will always be a bitter accusation, but this does not disturb its calm plastic Beauty; conversely, its plastic beauty enhances rather than hinders its emotional impact. The Spanish Civil War, a crucial moment in the period preceding World War II, broke out when *this* painter's life and *this* type of painting were approaching their decisive moment. The negative force of the brush was exhausting figurative painting and opening the door to systematic destruction.

At this period the figure was still intact, for the aim of experimentation was movement, the very quality that was to entail its disintegration. There was no need for violence to be hidden or transformed; it was simply identified with the disintegration of men brought about by their own bombs. Thus an experimental procedure resulted in a work whose singular meaning was that of a revolt and a denunciation of the massacre. The same social forces that had made the painter the negation of *their* order had also produced fascist acts of destruction and *Guernica.* This stroke

*Picasso's masterwork was painted in 1935, Goya's *Dos de Mayo* in 1808.

of fortune allowed Picasso to avoid cajoling beauty. If the crime is odious because it has become beautiful, this is attributable to the fact that it is "Explosive" and that the beauty of Picasso is "ordered exploding" (*explosante-fixe*), as Breton has said. The miraculous throw of the dice was never repeated. When Picasso tried, after World War II, to make a new beginning, his art had changed, and so had the world; they were now at odds. In short, censorship. When dealing with men and their suffering we can accept neither figuration of horror nor its disguise through pageantry.

For Lapoujade there is no longer any alternative; there is no longer any problem. This is because I borrowed the previous examples from figurative art. Paradoxically, imitation of the human figure entails externally imposed conditions while the absence of imitation entails conditions imposed by Art itself.

This is the last stage of a long journey. For years he has been depicting the nudes, couples, and crowds that have imposed themselves upon his brush. Look at his adolescents: nothing is missing. Yet the flesh is shown without its husk; the artificial contours of a body are not there. Nor is it strewn indiscriminately across the canvas. Contours, volume, mass, perspective — didn't he have to use all these to *put us in the presence* of a nude body? Evidently he did not. Or rather the reverse is true: the painting intrinsically requires us to experience the delicacy of flesh at the very moment when it is freed from alien forms.

The first stage is anxiety. Freed from an academic tradition, the artist wants to be able to cultivate thoroughly his garden — the plane surface that he has inherited — to transform routine farming which allows much of the land to lie fallow into intensive cultivation; furthermore, he wants to eliminate tolls and duties, barriers, detours, restrictions imposed by imitation. He wants to expand the scope of Art and at the same time to reaffirm its unity.

The fundamental purpose of experimentation is to give to Beauty a finer grain, a firmer and richer consistency. The artist's sole concern ought to be art. And when we look at Lapoujade's works, we feel not that he is searching for a new style of painting, but that he is giving another nature to painting. The rest follows,

64

of course. But serious changes in all the arts are at first material while form, the quintessential matter, comes last.

Lapoujade belongs to a generation of builders.[1] After what he himself calls the "disintegration of figurative art" by Picasso, Braque and a whole generation of analysts, all that remained for the newcomers was a medley of colors and rhythms, of crumbled remnants. They had no choice. These refined, ductile materials permitted and required integration into new wholes.

At first the newcomers were united by the common task that awaited them. Then each of them worked alone, trying to determine the aims and resources of the new art. Lapoujade chose to restore to us the World. This is in my opinion an option of capital importance. We can be sure, however, that the World made no requests; if it returned, bloody and new, its return was exacted by Painting.

Beauty is not monadic. It requires two unities, one visible and the other secret. If ever we managed even after relentless effort to penetrate into the essence of a work by a single glance, the object would be reduced to its inert visibility, Beauty would be effaced, and only its ornamentation would remain. To put it more aptly, the unification which the painter and the viewer seek can be achieved only through the permanent recomposition of a certain presence. And this presence, in turn, can communicate to us its indecomposable unity only through the medium of Art, and only in conjunction with our efforts and the painter's efforts to constitute or reconstitute the beauty of a whole.

The act is purely esthetic but, to the very degree that we remain aloof, the Whole infiltrates each visual synthesis, shaping it and giving it strength. *We* must rediscover the paths outlined for us by the painter and try to follow them. *We* must reconstruct these abrupt splotches of color, these distilled units of matter. *We* must

1. Occasionally one of these good painters remarks fatalistically that in a negative era their art destroys itself and refuses to be a medium of communication. But this is wrong. The new era builds more than it razes. Never before has painting been so compact, so concentrated as in the hands of these architects of the abstract.

revive echoes and rhythms. Only then does a presence, intuition denied, come to the rescue. By regulating our choice it keeps us moving along the right paths. To *construct* requires only the establishing of visible relations; to guarantee a construction and save it from total absurdity requires a transcendental unity. This unity insures that the viewer's eyes will never cease their movement, and the perpetual movement of the eyes accounts for the permanence of the invisible unity. We keep on looking, for if we ever stopped, everything would disintegrate.

What is this presence? I hasten to point out that Lapoujade is not a Platonist, nor am I. He is not guided in his compositions by an Idea. No, his guiding principle completes each canvas and is inseparable from it: neither can exist apart from the other. This abstract painter tries to imbue each painting with a concrete presence, and if all must be given the same name, then we might as well say that each work was motivated by a quest for meaning and that the quest was in each instance successful.

One point in particular merits clarification: a meaning is not a sign or a symbol — not even an image. When we view Canaletto's* painting of Venice, the resemblance is perfect. His "View of the Salute," which embodies both perfect perspective and topographic exactitude, cannot be misinterpreted. That is why the painting has no meaning. No more meaning than an Identification Card. When Guardi** shows scattered rubbish and bricks bathed in shimmering light, the alleys and canals that he has selected are insignificant. He shows us a commonplace wharf or a studied decomposition of light. Canaletto puts his brush in the service of his native town; Guardi is concerned only with plastic problems, with light and substance, with colors and light, with unity amid diversity through rigorous imprecision. Result: Venice is present in each canvas — as it was for him, as it is for

*The Italian painter and engraver Giovanni Antonio Canaletto (1697-1768) is noted for his precision as well as his fine sense of color and atmosphere.

**The landscapes of Francesco Guardi (1712-1793) are characterized by the dissolution of all figures into light and color.

us, as it has been experienced by everyone and seen by no one. I once paid a visit to a writer in the handsome garret of a brick palace beside a river. Not one of the figures that Guardi loved to paint was to be seen. Still, as soon as I saw the place, as soon as I observed my host's surroundings, my thoughts turned to the painter. I again saw his Venice, my Venice, the Venice experienced by each of us, and I felt the same way about other men, other objects and other places. The same? Not exactly. Meaning depends on the substance from which it emerges. Guardi always says more than we experience, and he says it differently.

Figurative painting was the first to be subjected to the rule of the two unities. Paradoxically, however, the incarnation of an invisible presence is obscured somewhat by an external bond — the brutal, mechanical bond that subjects the portrait to the model. The painter who incarnates himself in his work believes that grapes must be painted in clusters. It is as if since Apelles* the artist has had no ambition other than that of fooling the birds. Still, when Van Gogh painted a field, he did not pretend to transfer it to his canvas; he tried, through deceptive figuration whose sole criterion was the dictates of art, to incarnate on a sticky vertical surface the fullness of an immense world with its fields and men, including Van Gogh. Our world.

Not this: Van Gogh never tried to show us a field containing crows, and certainly not one containing fruit trees, for the simple reason that these objects resist figuration. He provides aesthetic substance for the incarnation of a presence that defies the brush: the world in the process of being covered with fields, its sap and flowers being poured *from a wand*. Again the image must be remote from the model or the world will not be as it should. Van Gogh had to begin by distorting everything if he was to show through art that the most delicate or innocent natural blemish is inseparable from horror.

We have seen that figurative painting involves three elements: the reality to be depicted on the canvas, the representation

---

*In the most famous of his portraits of Alexander the Great, his patron's hand appears to protrude from the colored surface.

provided by the painter, and the presence that finally permeates the work. This trinity might seem to entail complications, and it does. Though supposed to serve as a guide, our essentially ambiguous reality guides nothing; it floats around, bellies up, out of control; it can be manipulated only when real, that is, when transformed into an imaginary object. No field will transmit the charm or horror of the world until largely rebuilt; or rather it will transmit both, together or separately. It will reflect everything, but not consistently; instead of cohesiveness there will be fragmentation, absurdity, confusion.

Such monotonous disorder, unless restraints are introduced, will never transmit the complex structures of an *experienced* universe. What the painter adds to his canvas are the days of his life, the time that passes or does not pass. These powerful catalysts transform the object depicted. The inert individuality of the model is not transmitted to the canvas, but neither will the figure drawn there assume the general character of a type or sign. The influence of the world on a man and a man's enduring passion for the world will imbue a few acres of land with biographical individuality if both are recorded in the deceptive play of light on film. They will evoke the adventure of living, of contemplating the very birth of folly, of hurtling toward death.

The same chance figure, integrated for want of anything better into a composition, will undergo modifications imposed by art — it will be planed down, made smooth, reduced. Van Gogh pretends to "paint" a field but knows what he is really doing. He brings order to a canvas but never tries to reconstruct with exactitude the soft ripples made by the wind in passing through wheat or to evoke completely the staggering, intimate presence of man, the heart of the world, through that part of the world, the heart of man, that he has circumscribed.

When finally he puts down his palette, when the presence is incarnated in the composition, what has become of the representation of the object? A transparency, a trace, little more than a magnificent allusion to the object represented. And the field, finally, the plain field that the artist has pretended to represent, this would be eliminated from the canvas if the world did not come to the rescue and incarnate itself in the undulating expanses of wheat bereft of figures, in the thick paste of a rimless sun or in the galaxy of suns at earth-level which are the only true inhabitants of the canvas and the only true vestiges of the creative act.

In figurative painting conventions are of little importance. It is sufficient if we are convinced that the figure proposed is in *this* system of references the best representation of the object. The best means the strongest, richest, most meaningful form. A matter of luck or skill. Still, since the last century each new option has tended to widen the gap between figure and object. The greater the distance between the two, the stronger the inner tension of the work. When the artist goes so far as to discard resemblances, to rule out any similitude between image and reality other than a fortuitous one, meaning is set free by the disintegration of *representation* and begins to exert a negative influence. Meaning is the product of the forces of destruction. It flashes out across dissemblances, lacunae, approximations, deliberate indeterminations. Invisible, it blinds because it dissolves the figures in its inimitable presence.

Such also are the meanings that haunt our world. They annihilate detail and draw from it their sustenance. Every brick wall hides Venice from me if it is alone. I will still sense this city even after its palaces have been destroyed and its plumage plucked and redeployed in such a way that I lose sight of every feather. On his canvas the artist paints the rudiments of intuition only to blot them out immediately thereafter. Aroused by this refusal the presence — which is the thing itself undetailed and in undivided space — will incarnate itself. But this is a trap set by the artist. He introduces other figures that bear no relation to the object in question but suggest other associations — waste paper, sand, pebbles. He seeks to produce a new being, a presence all the more austere because it feeds on an absence surreptitiously falsified by substitutions. How many painters between World War I and World War II dreamed of being at once chemists and alchemists, capable of forcing lead to fuse with gold and be incarnated with its essence? One of them, aiming at a double transformation, tried to paint a wardrobe that would be a chest without ceasing to be a wardrobe; he hoped that elective signalizing would allow him to treat each object by turns as plastic substance or as incarnation.

This double aim was always suspect. The artist wanted, not to annihilate and make us experience the world's disheveled meanings, but to create meanings that had never before existed. Abortive marvels, uninspired legerdemain. At the end of this long crisis in which the artist's creativity was submerged in disillusionment through failure to understand that the imaginary is the sole absolute, the figure had the good sense to disintegrate. And meaning? Did it disappear at the same time? Quite the opposite. As we have just seen, there was no true link between the two. Set free, the incarnate presence appeared as the *sine qua non* of abstract art.

The shattering and scattering of images is not a studied choice exercised by new painters. It is an event that is still unfolding, and not all of its consequences are known. A permanent deflagration, it spreads continuously from canvas to canvas. Each painter sees it simultaneously as his problem and his material. Art offers him an explosion to subdue, and this through explosive tactics.

Their predecessors having sown the wind, those who today seek to subdue the storm stir up a cyclone within the cyclone and organize its tiniest spangles with pitiless rigor. Using the laws that they have devised and visual logic, they must preserve and reshape this pulverulence; search for the multiple unity within the multiplicity; acquire new insights into the canvas; know how to detail and contain on it dilations and coagulations, whirling fields of fire, dark commas, splotches, puddles, trails of blood across the sun; use fluidity and density as rigid structural elements in a unified plastic ceremony. Deceit and trickery are out. Details are no longer negligible; nothing is missing, everything counts.

By toying with colors, strengthening lines, making and exploiting discoveries, structuring the whirlwind, and compensating for local turbulences by balancing them rigorously, the painter causes the formidable event to coagulate. At the worst, the result is a rose-window; at best, a pleasant carousal. To preserve the rhythm

70

of explosive space, to prolong the vibration of its colors, to exploit in depth the strange, terrifying disintegration of being and its whirling movement, the artist must use his brush to impose meaning on his canvas and on us.

No movement without roads, no roads without direction — and who will decide these vectorial determinations unless the artist has an unrestricted view? But he must catch sight of a mighty motif if he is to undertake the unification of this sumptuous dispersion without figures and resemblances. Only one motif exists: the secret unity of the work. It is, if you will, in the painting itself.

There is another world, said Eluard, and it is in this one. But the artist will find it only by proceeding towards the unification of his canvas. Each time that we effect new syntheses or that the eye unifies neighboring objects, we become a little more aware of its presence. We can never expose all of this presence, for it is merely the work itself considered as an organism. Lapoujade was invited by Art to duplicate the false unity of figurative painting; as soon as he did, he understood what was required of him: to eliminate chance and give to an infinitely divisible surface the indivisible unity of a whole.

A few painters feel as he does and have chosen lyrical unity. The lyrical painter impulsively attacks his canvas; he leaves it to attack us. He paints as he strikes, and the presence incarnated on his canvas is his own. He gives to his work the quick unity of an aggressive act. Lapoujade knows that lyrical painting is possible. It can be done and has already been done. He might be afraid that a projection of himself in the pure medium of art would be illegible. And of course Art, in spite of what is too often said about it, is not a language. But neither is it true that we communicate only through signs. We *experience* through others what others *experience* as us; for our fellow men we are a common experience.

Lyrical painters try to give to their canvas the unity of their emotion, of their élan or their calm; in short, they choose to make the viewing public experience their singular adventure. Would this be possible without preliminary unanimity? Probably not, for singularity is revealed only as a differentiation from commonality. If painters only had to paint themselves, each could have his day. Art would preserve its integrity even if hermetic. But lyrical painting is also an act affixing to multiplicity an indispensable seal, and this act must be forever renewed. Beauty is not created unless the act is renewed.

Since the eye has as its immediate stimulus communication, representing the incessantly recreated completion and perpetual animation of the abstract work, the painter must give it his immediate and constant attention. Meaning, since it is revealed through unification and since its revelation promotes unity, must be by nature communicable. To establish the condition without providing the means for fulfilling it is to risk exposing the work to the perils of indetermination.

Such is, I believe, the profound conviction of Lapoujade. Painting is an important avenue of communication, and at every intersection it finds the presences that it incarnates. Nor does it have to search them out. Meanings, if the artist wishes to collect them, can be gathered by the dozens; the eye may read them, but slowly, without particular awareness of their obviousness or necessity. If they are not evoked at once by the trembling of matter taking shape and the urgency shared by painter and viewer, how can they be imposed? False evidence is misleading; the artist lends a hand and sets us straight. If without even lending an ear he understands the confused sounds of highways and byways, this is because he too, is a highway. And here and there are neglected, deserted trails. Lapoujade, the versatile link between man and the world, paints teeming, stampeding masses as they cry out, fall silent, remain mysteriously suspended, and stubbornly dissolve into asphalt coloration. He insists that solitude does not befit painting and his canvases have convinced me that he is right.

One day, said Marx, there will be no more painters. It would be just as fitting that one day there will be neither men nor painters, but that day is remote. Lapoujade is a strange contradiction. With a few of his contemporaries he has reduced painting to the sumptuous austerity of its essence; surrounded by human presences incarnated on his canvas, however, he is the first not to claim special privileges. A painter, he uses painting to tear away the artist's mask, leaving only men and himself, without prerogatives, one among us, obliterated by the splendor of his work.

Look at his works: crowds. Nor is he the first, for the more fools people see on a canvas, the more they are accustomed to laugh. But the old artists were protected. They worked at the right hand of the Prince and on a tribune; if they had to work face to face with the people and on their level, then they were protected by soldiers. Each painting conveyed its message: "I am a painter; I belong to you, great men of the World, and I show you the superficial side of the mob which you govern and from which you have deigned to rescue me forever."

The age was responsible and so was the "figure." How was the artist to paint the crowd seen by itself, as it experienced itself and makes itself, here and everywhere? How was he to curve space to inscribe in it the infinite circle whose center is everywhere entwined with its circumference? How was he to show in each the leaders and the followers? And these human molecules, what forms, what colors would show that each defies comparison with the others and that all are interchangeable? What system of references could he choose to make lovers of art understand that the crowd can admit the painter into their ranks only by stripping him bare, that he is denied the flimsiest prop or visual accessory, that aroused masses reject seconds, that he must enter their ranks naked, unadorned, as a man, participate in everything, flee or change, provide disciplined leadership, be put to the test, produce. Was he to bear the weight of twenty or a hundred thousand other "selfs" only to return to his canvas, under the best possible circumstances, with violent but inchoate memories? The inner reactions of a crowd cannot be seen. They are assimilated, experienced, acknowledged. Let that be represented through figures!

This is what characterizes the new painter of crowds: he can incarnate their presence only by refusing to represent them through figures. Of course, by banishing the Figure from his studio he like all artists is renewing the vow of penury that Beauty has never ceased to exact and will never cease to exact. But he goes much further than this: he gives up his tribune. A man, he refuses to be excluded by virtue of his privileged position and to contemplate his species from the outside. Figurative painting isolates both painter and model. While deforming the figure, anarchistic and bourgeois artists spoke with gentle irony of their solitude. Obviously, they were not communicating!

There is instantaneous communication, however, if the artist is Lapoujade. His crowd is real, surging, uneasy. He is *exposed* to it and following the gradual annihilation of detail, there remains the meaning of the mass rally, of the police charge of October 27. The meaning is the experience shared by thousands of unknown people certain that for all of them it was the same. This experience requires substance for its incarnation; language is inadequate since it isolates a vast number of facts each of which draws its meaning from the others.

To express, to paint his indeterminate and multiple adventure as an interchangeable man, Lapoujade provides for crowds a substance which, though fluid, manifests rigid unity within dispersion. The unification of discrete particles is the realization of a transcendent element: the explosive unity of the masses. It follows that the crowd within each of us is urged to rediscover the discrete totality of its life. The painter leads us. There are, he says, immediate data of expression: the dark, dense aggregation of colors at the bottom of the canvas, a swelling of matter, a vivid upsurge of light, a hundred other, a thousand other interlocking constituents. But they only stir the heart. The essential quality is in the singularity of the routes traced by his brush. Now compact, now rarefied, at times thick and at other times liquid, the substance itself is not intended to reveal the invisible, the metamorphosis around us and through us of a glade into a thicket, a steppe, or a virgin forest. It *suggests* through its texture and its itineraries.

The painter uses to advantage the contrast between the rigidity of his materials and the indeterminacy of experience. Crowded spots seem to recoil from each other; a new route, suddenly discovered, forces colors to pale as they acquire new reciprocal relations; finally, through these metamorphoses we grasp the

74

indivisible presence of the manifestation as it is incarnated with all its densities at one and the same time. And then, abruptly, a path of asphalt: space. It overflows and runs down to the bottom of the canvas. But is there a top? A bottom?

Space itself is *a direction* created by the crowd and determined by their actions. The splotch of color is a thick spurt, a flight to the horizon, an abrupt penetration of space. The police charge. Will the people flee? Resist? No matter what they do, space exists with all its dimensions in one. It is distance — diminishing on one side and on the other appearing interminable. But words are unnecessary; the splotch is able by itself to revive meaning. And what is created is not an artificial presence, a wardrobe-fish or a wolf-table as in the time of trick artists, but a real presence, indivisible, common and singular, enriched by everything contributed by the painter.

Man among men, men in the midst of the world, the world within men, that is the unique presence evoked by his overpowering explosion; that is the unique ordeal, common to all and yet peculiar to each, experienced along with us, through us and for us by Lapoujade; that is the unique message communicated at first glance to illuminate the canvas even before being illuminated by it. But the rejection of special privilege, identical to the rejection of figuration, is a commitment made by painter and by man. It led Lapoujade from one canvas to another toward the most radical consequences of this undertaking.

To begin with, if the painter ceases to contemplate other men, if he is rejected by his peers, *action* sets him apart or constitutes a permanent bond with all men and each man. He acts, suffers, frees himself and dominates or is dominated. His act of contemplation is purely passive; his brush must recreate action, not from without but through his experiencing the Other. The Meaning of the painting will be the incarnation of the Other known through the modification that he is subjected to and of the painter as he discovers himself through the modification that he experiences or inflicts.

Whatever its carnation, the inertia of a Nude is generally distressing. The woman is alone, the painter at the opposite end of the room. In real life no one — certainly no painter — ever contemplated so docile a nude from so far away. Lapoujade paints a couple. He has at times evoked the tenderness of adolescent flesh, but in the erotic series called "Le Vif du Sujet" he wanted to suggest woman as she is approached by men, as she appears in the act of love. A Nude, in short, involves two people. Even if the only real presence is a woman, the presence of a man is suggested by the movement of colors, and this gives to the canvas *its* presence.

Action, the multiple link between men, molds splotches of color and matter into a coherent structure and brings to perfection the painter's project: to use the visible splendors of nonfigurative art to incarnate that which cannot be represented through figures. Abstract art, which seemed at first to impose limitations, actually extends the painter's freedom and assigns to him new functions.

The other consequence of this option is obviously the unprivileged painter's decision to show his solidarity with other men. Their solidarity has a firm basis, for he has only what they have, wants nothing more, is nothing more. Then, too, its permanence is assured. Woman appears on his canvases in the act of love, men joined in a common struggle. The most astounding yet simple truth is that the choice of abstraction led Lapoujade in the name of art itself once again to place man on his canvases. Not, however, as man appeared in the days of princes and prelates — modest and anonymous in his patient and tenacious struggle to satisfy his hunger and deliver himself from oppression. He appears everywhere on the canvases of Lapoujade, who never ceases painting him and refining his portrait.

Lapoujade now understands that man, seen by an unprivileged eye, is today neither great nor small, beautiful nor ugly. His art challenges him to place on his canvases a true portrait of the human kingdom, and the truth about this kingdom, today, is that the human species includes torturers, their accomplices and martyrs. Torturers are few in number but their accomplices are many; most people fall into the group of the tortured, or are candidates for torture. Lapoujade understands this. No one in 1961 can speak of men without first mentioning torturers; no one can speak of Frenchmen to the French without mentioning the tortured Algerians. That is our portrait; we must look at it realistically; later we can decide to preserve it or to modify it.

Lapoujade chose to show torture because it is deeply ingrained in us, because it reaches, alas, to our ignoble core. On attempting to paint it, he saw that he could capture its portrait only through nonfigurative art, which evokes the total meaning of the human situation. His triptych is beautiful without reserve — and can be beautiful without remorse. Beauty is not hidden in nonfigurative painting. It shows through. The painting *exhibits* nothing. It lets horror seep down but *only if it is beautiful* — that is, organized in the most complex and fertile manner.

The preciseness of the scenes evoked depends on the preciseness of his brush. The viewer must identify and reconstruct the conjugation of striae and beautiful yet sinister colors; this is the only way of *experiencing* the meaning of what was for Alleg and Djamila their martyrdom.*

Meaning, as I have said, contributes to the total picture something other than a new and alien element. Incarnated in plastic substance, it allows us to sense, through the frenzy of colors, mutilated flesh and unbearable suffering. But the suffering that we sense is that of the victims, and let us not pretend that we find it unbearable in this imperious and discreet form.

Behind and through the radiant Beauty we see only a pitiless Destiny which men — we men — have made for man. Lapoujade's success is complete because it issues from painting and its laws. In other words, it conforms to the logic of abstract painting. It is no mean achievement, I believe, for a painter to meet with such favor in our eyes by showing undisguised the grief that wells from our hearts.

*Henri Alleg was charged with attempting to endanger state security and imprisoned after he published a book detailing tortures to which he had allegedly been subjected as a prisoner of French troops in Algeria. His book, later published in English as *The Question*, was banned in France in 1958. Djamila Bouhired, Algeria's Joan of Arc, was tortured and sentenced to die. She was reprieved only after her plight became an international scandal.

THE MOBILES OF CALDER*

The sculptor is supposed to imbue something immobile with movement, but it would be wrong to compare Calder's art with the sculptor's. Calder captures movement rather than suggests it; he has no intention of entombing it forever in bronze or gold, those glorious, asinine materials that are by nature immobile. With vile, inconsistent substances, with tiny slivers of bone or tin or zinc, he fashions strange arrangements of stems and branches, of rings and feathers and petals. They are resonators or traps; they dangle at the end of a fine wire like a spider at the end of its silk thread or settle on a pedestal, wan, exhausted, feigning sleep; a passing tremor strikes them, animates them, is canalized by them and given a fugitive form—a *Mobile* is born.

A Mobile: a small local festival, an object defined by its movement and nonexistent apart from it, a flower that withers as soon as it stops moving, a free play of movement, like coruscating light. Sometimes Calder amuses himself by imitating a new form. For example, he once presented me with a bird of paradise with iron wings; a wisp of air brushing it while escaping through the window is enough to rouse the bird; it clicks, stands erect, spins, nods its crested head, rolls and pitches and then, as if in sudden obedience to an unseen signal, executes a slow

*First published in *Les Temps Modernes* and later in *Situations III* (Paris: Gallimard), 1948. Alexander Calder achieved recognition as a sculptor some twenty years ago when the Museum of Modern Art exhibited his works. His mobiles are today found in such diverse places as New York's Chase Manhattan Bank, a hotel in Cincinnati, an airport in Pittsburgh, and UNESCO headquarters in Paris. He maintains two studio-homes, one near Saché, France, and the other near Roxbury, Connecticut.

turn with its wings spread. But most of the time it imitates nothing, and I know no other art less deceptive than his.

Sculpture suggests movement, painting depth or light. Calder suggests nothing; he captures and embellishes true, living movements. His mobiles signify nothing, refer to nothing other than themselves; they simply are, they are absolutes.

In his mobiles chance probably plays a greater part than in any other creation of man. The forces at work are too numerous and too complicated for any human mind, even that of their creator, to foresee all possible combinations. For each of them Calder establishes a general scheme of movement, then abandons it; the time, the sun, heat and wind will determine each particular dance. Thus the object is always midway between the servility of statues and the independence of natural events. Each of his evolutions is an inspiration of the moment; it reveals his general theme but permits a thousand personal variations. It is a little hot-jazz tune, unique and ephemeral, like the sky, like the morning; if you miss it, you will have lost it forever.*

Valéry said that the sea is a perpetual renewal. One of Calder's objects is like the sea — and equally spellbinding: ever changing, always new. A passing glance is not enough; one must live with it and be bewitched by it. Then the imagination can revel in pure, ever-changing forms — forms that are at once free and fixed.

The movements of the object are intended only to please us, to titillate our eyes, but they have a profound, metaphysical meaning. The reason is that the mobiles have to have some source of mobility. Previously Calder used an electric motor; he now abandons his mobiles in the midst of nature; in a garden or near an open window, they vibrate in the wind like aeolian harps. Fed on air, they respire and draw their life from the tenuous life of the atmosphere. Thus their mobility is of very peculiar kind.

Although they are human creations, they never have the pre-

---

*In Sartre's earliest novel, *Nausea* (first published in 1938), jazz enables the central character to escape momentarily from the pervasive, overpowering feeling of nausea that engulfs him.

cision and efficiency of movement of Vaucanson's automatons.*
But the charm of the automaton resides in the fact that it agitates
a fan or plays a guitar like a man, yet moves its hand with the
blind, persistent rigor of purely mechanical translations. Against
this, Calder's mobiles move and hesitate, as if correcting a mistake
by starting anew.

I have seen in his studio a beater and a gong suspended high
overhead; the slightest gust caused the beater to pursue the gong
as it turned round; it would take aim, lash out at the gong, miss
it by a hair, like an awkward hand, and then when least expected,
strike and hit it squarely in the center, producing a frightening
noise. But the movements are too artistically contrived to be
compared with those of a ball rolling on a uneven plane and
changing its course solely on the basis of irregularities encountered.
They have a life of their own.

One day when I was talking with Calder in his studio, a
model which until then had remained at rest was seized, right
in my presence, by a violent agitation. I retreated until I thought
I was beyond its reach. Suddenly, just when the agitation had
ceased and the model seemed lifeless, its long, majestic tail, which
had not moved previously, indolently roused, as if regretfully,
rotated in the air and grazed my nose.

Their hesitations, revivals, gropings, fumblings, abrupt decisions,
and especially their marvelous swan-like nobility make of Calder's
mobiles strange creatures, halfway between matter and life. Sometimes their movements seem to have a purpose and sometimes
they seem to have lost their purpose along the way and to have
lapsed into imbecile fluctuations. My bird flies, wavers, swims
like a swan, like a frigate; he is a bird, a single bird and then,
suddenly, he falls apart and all that remains are slivers of metal
traversed by vain little tremors.

Calder's mobiles, which are neither completely living nor completely mechanical and which constantly change but always return

*Jacques de Vaucanson (1709-1782) devised mechanisms that brought him
considerable fame. Among his most celebrated automatons were his *Flute
Player* and *Duck*.

80

to their original position are like aquatic plants bent low by a stream, the petals of the sensitive plant, the legs of a headless frog, or gossamer caught in an updraft. In short, although Calder has no desire to imitate anything—his one aim is to create chords and cadences of unknown movements—his mobiles are at once lyrical inventions, technical, almost mathematical combinations and the perceptible symbol of Nature: great elusive Nature, squandering pollen and abruptly causing a thousand butterflies to take wing and never revealing whether she is the blind concatenation of causes and effects or the gradual unfolding, forever retarded, disconcerted and thwarted, of an Idea.

THE QUEST FOR THE ABSOLUTE*

A glance at Giacometti's antediluvian face reveals his arrogance and his desire to place himself at the beginning of time. He ridicules Culture and has no faith in Progress — not in the Fine Arts, at least. He considers himself no further "advanced" than his adopted contemporaries, the men of Eyzies and Altamira.** Then, when nature and men were in their prime, there was neither ugliness nor beauty, neither taste nor dilettantes nor criticism. The man who first had the notion of carving a man from a block of stone had to start from zero.

His model: man. Neither a dictator nor a general nor an athlete, primitive man still lacked the dignity and charm that would seduce future sculptors. He was nothing more than a long, indistinct silhouette walking across the horizon. But his movements were perceptibly different from the movements of things; they emanated from him like first beginnings and impregnated the air with signs of an ethereal future. They must be understood in terms of their ends — to pick a berry or push aside a briar — not their origins. They could never be isolated or localized.

I can separate a bent branch from a tree but never an upraised arm or a clinched fist from a man. The *man* raises his arm, the *man* clinches his fist, the *man* is the indissoluble unit and the absolute source of his movements. Furthermore, he is an enchanter of signs; they cling to his hair, shine in his eyes, dance between

*First published in *Les Temps Modernes* and later reprinted in *Situations III* (Paris: Gallimard), 1948.

**That the paleolithic hunters of southern France and Northern Spain had a keenly developed aesthetic sense is attested by many artifacts preserved in limestone caves near Eyzies-de-Tayac and Altamira.

his lips, perch on his fingertips. He speaks with his whole body; when he runs he speaks, when he talks he speaks, and when he falls asleep his sleep is speech.

His substance: a rock, a lump of space. From mere space Giacometti therefore had to fashion a man, to inscribe movement in total immobility, unity in infinite multiplicity, the absolute in pure relativity, the future in the eternal present, the loquacity of signs in the tenacious silence of things. The gap between substance and model seems unbridgeable, yet exists only because Giacometti has gauged its dimensions. I am not sure whether he is a man bent on imposing a human seal on space or a rock dreaming of human qualities. Or perhaps he is both and mediates between the two.

The sculptor's passion is to transform himself completely into length so that from its fullness can spill the statue of a man. He is haunted by thoughts of stone. Once he was terrified by the void; for months he walked to and fro, accompanied by an abyss — his emptiness in the process of achieving awareness of its desolate sterility. On another occasion it seemed to him that objects, spiritless and dead, were no longer touching the ground; he lived in a fluctuating universe, knowing in his flesh and even to the point of martyrdom that there is neither height nor depth nor length nor real contact between things; but at the same time he was aware that the sculptor's task is to carve from the infinite archipelago a face filled with the only being that can *touch* other beings.

I know no one else who is as sensitive as he to the magic of faces and gestures. He looks at them with passionate envy, as if they were from another kingdom. At his wit's end he has at times tried to mineralize his equals: to envision crowds advancing blindly toward him, rolling across boulevards like stones in an avalanche. Thus each of his obsessions was a task, an experience, a means of experiencing space.

"He's crazy," people say. "Sculptors have been carving away for three thousand years — and nicely, too — without such rigmaroles. Why doesn't he try to produce impeccable works according

83

to tested techniques instead of pretending to ignore his predecessors?"

The truth is that for three thousand years sculptors have been carving only cadavers. Sometimes they are shown reclining on tombs; sometimes they are seated on curule chairs or perched on horses. But a dead man on a dead horse does not make even half a living creature. He deceives the rigid, wide-eyed people in the Museum. His arms pretend to move but are held fast by iron shanks at each end; his rigid outlines can hardly contain infinite dispersion; mystified by a crude resemblance, the spectator allows his imagination to imbue the eternal sinking of matter with movement, heat and light.

It is therefore necessary to start again from zero. After three thousand years the task of Giacometti and of contemporary sculptors is not to glut galleries with new works but to prove that sculpture is possible by carving. To prove that sculpture is possible just as by walking Diogenes proved to Parmenides and Zeno the possibility of movement. It is necessary to go the limit and see what can be done. If the undertaking should end in failure, it would be impossible to decide under even the most favorable circumstances whether this meant the failure of the sculptor or of sculpture; others would come along, and they would have to begin anew. Giacometti himself is forever beginning anew. But involved here is more than an infinite progression; there is a fixed boundary to be reached, a unique problem to be resolved: how to make a man out of stone without petrifying him. All or nothing: if the problem is solved, the number of statues is of little consequence.

"If I only knew how to make one," says Giacometti, "I could make them by the thousands. . . ." Until he succeeds, there will be no statues at all but only rough hewings that interest Giacometti only insofar as they bring him closer to his goal. He shatters everything and begins anew. From time to time his friends manage to save from destruction a head, a young woman, an adolescent. He raises no objection and again takes up his task. In fifteen years he has had but one exposition.

He consented to the exposition because he had to make a living, but even then he had misgivings and wrote by way of

84

excusing himself: "It is mainly because I was goaded by the terror of poverty that these sculptures exist in this state (bronzed and photographed), but I am not quite sure of them; still, they were almost what I wanted. Almost."

What bothers him is that these impressive works, always mediating between nothingness and being, always in the process of modification, perfection, destruction and renewal, have begun to exist independently and in earnest, and have made a start, far from him, toward a social career. He prefers simply to forget about them. The remarkable thing about him is his intransigence in his quest for the absolute.

This active, determined worker is displeased by the resistance of stone, which slows down his movements. He has chosen a weightless substance which is also the most ductile, perishable and spiritual of all substances — plaster. He hardly feels it at his fingertips; it is the impalpable reflex of his movements.

One first notices in his studio strange scare-crows made of white daubs that coagulate around long reddish strings. His experiences, his ideas, his desires and his dreams project themselves for a moment on his plaster men, give them a form and pass on, and their form passes on with them. Each of these nebulous creatures undergoing perpetual metamorphosis seems like Giacometti's very life transcribed in another language.

Maillol's statues insolently fling in our eyes their heavy eternity. But the eternity of stone is synonymous with inertia; it is the present forever solidified. Giacometti never speaks of eternity, never thinks of eternity. I was pleased by what he had said to me one day concerning some statues that he had just destroyed: "I was happy with them, but they were made to last only a few hours."

A few hours — like the dawn, like sadness, like ephemera. And his creations, because they were destined to perish on the very night of their birth, are the only ones among all the sculptures that I know to retain the ineffable charm of transiency. Never was substance less eternal, more fragile, more nearly human. Giacometti's substance — this strange flour that slowly settles over his studio and buries it, that seeps under his nails and into the deep wrinkles on his face — is the dust of space.

But space, even if naked, is still superfluity. Giacometti is terrified by the infinite. Not by Pascalian infinity, not by what is infinitely great. The infinity that runs through his fingers is of a more subtle and secretive type. In space, says Giacometti, there is a superfluity. This *superfluity* is the pure and simple coexistence of juxtaposed elements. Most sculptors have allowed themselves to be deceived; they have confused the proliferation of space with generosity, they have put too much into their works, they have been captivated by the plump contour of a marble bosom, they have unfolded, stuffed and distended the human gesture.

Giacometti knows that there is nothing superfluous about a living person because everything is function. He knows that space is a cancer that destroys being, that devours everything. For him, to sculpture -is to trim the fat from space, to compress it and wring from it all its exteriority. The attempt may well seem hopeless, and I believe that on two or three occasions Giacometti has reached the verge of despair. If sculpturing entails carving and patching in this incompressible medium, then sculpture is impossible. "And yet," he said, "if I begin my statue, like others, at the tip of the nose, it will not be too great an infinity of time before I reach the nostril." Then it was that he made his discovery.

Consider Ganymede on his pedestal. If you ask me how far away he is, I will tell you that I don't know what you are talking about. By "Ganymede" do you mean the youth carried away by Jupiter's eagle? If so, I will say that there is no *real* distance between us, that no such relation exists because he does not exist. Or are you referring to the block of marble that the sculptor fashioned in the image of the handsome lad? If so, we are dealing with something real, with an existing mineral, and can draw comparisons.

Painters have long understood all that since in pictures the unreality of the third dimension necessarily entails the unreality of the two other dimensions. If follows that the distance between the figures and my eyes is *imaginary*. If I advance, I move nearer to the canvas, not to them. Even if I put my nose on them, I would still see them twenty steps away since for me they exist once and for all at a distance of twenty steps. It follows also that painting is not subject to Zeno's line of reasoning; even if I bisected the space separating the Virgin's foot from St. Joseph's foot, and the resulting halves again and again to infinity, I would simply be dividing a certain length on the canvas, not flagstones supporting the Virgin and her husband.

Sculptors failed to recognize these elementary truths because they were working in a three-dimensional space on a real block of marble and, although the product of their art was an imaginary man, they thought that they were working with real dimensions. The confusion of real and unreal space had curious results. In the first place, instead of reproducing what they *saw* — that is, a model ten steps away — they reproduced in clay what *was* — that is, the model itself. Since they wanted their statue to give to the spectator standing ten steps away the impression that the model had given them, it seemed logical to make a figure that would be for him what the model had been for them; and that was possible only if the marble was *here* just as the model had been *out there*.

But what exactly is the meaning of being *here* and *out there?* Ten steps away from her, I form a certain image of a nude woman; if I approach and look at her at close range, I no longer recognize her; the craters, crevices, cracks, the rough, black herbs, the greasy streaks, the lunar orography in its entirety simply can not be the smooth, fresh skin I was admiring from a distance. Is that what the sculptor should imitate? There would be no end to his task, and besides, no matter how close he came to her face, he could always narrow the gap still further.

It follows that a statue truly resembles neither what the model *is* nor what the sculptor *sees*. It is constructed according to certain contradictory conventions, for the sculptor represents certain details not visible from so far away under the pretext that they exist and neglects certain others that do exist under the pretext that they are unseen. What does this mean other than

87

that he takes the viewpoint of the spectator in order to reconstruct an acceptable figure? But if so, my relation to Ganymede varies with my position; if near, I will discover details which escaped me at a distance. And this brings us to the paradox: I have *real* relations with an illusion; or, if you prefer, my true distance from the block of marble has been confused with my imaginary distance from Ganymede.

The result of all this is that the properties of true space overlay and mask those of imaginary space. Specifically, the real divisibility of marble destroys the indivisibility of the person. Stone and Zeno are the victors. Thus the classical sculptor flirts with dogmatism because he thinks that he can eliminate his own look and imbue something other than man with human nature; but the truth is that he does not know what he is doing since he does not reproduce what he sees. In his search for truth he encounters convention. And since the net result is to shift to the visitor the responsibility for breathing life into his inert images, his quest for the absolute finally makes his work depend on the relativity of the angles from which it is viewed. As for the spectator, he takes the imaginary for the real and the real for the imaginary; he searches for indivisibility and everywhere finds divisibility.

By reversing classicism, Giacometti has restored to statues an imaginary, indivisible space. His unequivocal acceptance of relativity has revealed the absolute. The fact is that he was the first to sculpture man as he is seen — from a distance. He confers *absolute distance* on his images just as the painter confers absolute distance on the inhabitants of his canvas. He creates a figure "ten steps away" or "twenty steps away," and do what you will, it remains there. The result is a leap into the realm of the unreal since its relation to you no longer depends on your relation to the block of plaster — the liberation of Art.

A classical statue must be studied or approached if it is continuously to reveal new details; first, parts are singled out, then parts of parts, etc. with no end in sight. You can't approach one of Giacometti's sculptures. Don't expect a belly to expand as you draw near it; it will not change and you on moving away will have the strange impression of marking time. We have a vague feeling, we conjecture, we are on the point of seeing nipples on the breasts; one or two steps closer and we are still expectant; one more step and everything vanishes. All that remains are plaits of plaster. His statues can be viewed only from a respectful distance. Still, everything is there: whiteness, roundness, the elastic sagging of a beautiful ripe belly. Everything except matter. From twenty steps we only think we see the wearisome desert of adipose tissue; it is suggested, outlined, indicated, but not given.

Now we know what press Giacometti used to condense space. There could be but one — distance. He placed distance within our reach by showing us a distant woman who keeps her distance even when we touch her with our fingertips. The breasts that we envisioned and anticipated will never be exposed, for they are but expectancy; the bodies that he creates have only enough substance to hold forth a promise.

"That's impossible," someone might say. "The same object can't be viewed from close range and from afar." But we are not speaking of the same object; the block of plaster is near, the imaginary person far away.

"Even so, distance would still have to compress all three dimensions, and here length and depth are affected while height remains intact." True. But it is also true that each man in the eyes of other men possesses absolute dimensions. As a man walks away from me, he does not seem to grow smaller; his qualities seem rather to condense while his "figure" remains intact. As he draws near me, he does not grow larger but his qualities expand.

Admittedly, however, Giacometti's men and women are closer to us in height than in width — as if they are projecting their stature. But Giacometti purposely elongated them. We must understand that his creatures, which are wholly and immediately what they are, can neither be studied nor observed. As soon as I see them, I know them; they flood my field of vision as an idea floods my mind; the idea has the same immediate translucidity and is instantaneously wholly what it is. Thus Giacometti has found a unique solution to the problem of unity within multiplicity by simply suppressing multiplicity.

Plaster and bronze are divisible, but a woman in motion has the indivisibility of an idea or an emotion; she has no parts because she surrenders herself simultaneously. To give perceptible expression to pure presence, to surrender of self, to instantaneous emergence, Giacometti has recourse to elongation.

The original movement of creation — the timeless, indivisible movement so beautifully epitomized by long, gracile legs — shoots through his Greco-like bodies and lifts them toward the heavens. In them even more than in one of Praxiteles' athletes I recognize man, the first cause, the absolute source of movement. Giacometti succeeded in giving to his substance the only truly human unity — unity of action.

Such is the type of Copernican revolution that Giacometti has attempted to introduce into sculpture. Before him men thought that they were sculpturing *being,* and this absolute dissolved into an infinite number of appearances. He chose to sculpture *situated* appearance and discovered that this was the path to the absolute. He exposes to us men and women as *already seen* but not as already seen by himself alone. His figures are already seen just as a foreign language that we are trying to learn is already spoken. Each of them reveals to us man as he is seen, as he is for other men, as he emerges in interhuman surroundings — not, as I said earlier for the sake of simplification, ten or twenty steps away, but at a man's distance. Each of them offers proof that man *is* not at first in order to be *seen* afterwards but that he is the being whose essence is in his existence for others. When I perceive the statue of a woman, I find that my congealed look is drawn to it, producing in me a pleasing uneasiness. I feel constrained, yet know neither why nor by whom until I discover that I am constrained to see and constrained by myself.

Furthermore, Giacometti often takes pleasure in adding to our perplexity — for example by placing a distant head on a nearby body so that we no longer know where to begin or exactly how to behave. But even without such complications his ambiguous images are disconcerting, for they upset our most cherished visual habits. We have long been accustomed to smooth, mute creatures fashioned for the purpose of curing us of the sickness of having a

90

body; these guardian spirits have watched over the games of our childhood and bear witness in our gardens to the notion that the world is without risks, that nothing ever happens to anyone and, consequently, that the only thing that ever happened to them was death at birth.

Against this, something obviously has happened to Giacometti's bodies. Are they emerging from a concave mirror, from a fountain of youth or from a deportation camp? We seem at first glance to be confronted by the emaciated martyrs of Buchenwald. But almost immediately we realize our mistake. His thin, gracile creatures rise toward the heavens and we discover a host of Ascensions and Assumptions; they dance, they *are* dances, made of the same rarefied substance as the glorious bodies promised us. And while we are still contemplating the mystical upsurge, the emaciated bodies blossom and we see only terrestrial flowers.

The martyred creature was only a woman but she was *all* woman — glimpsed, furtively desired, retreating in the distance with the comic dignity of fragile, gangling girls walking lazily from bed to bathroom in their high-heeled shoes and with the tragic horror of scarred victims of a holocaust or famine; all woman — exposed, rejected, near, remote; all woman — with traces of hidden leanness showing through alluring plumpness and hideous leanness mollified by suave plumpness; all woman — in danger here on earth but no longer entirely on earth, living and relating to us the astounding adventure of flesh, *our* adventure. For she chanced to be born, like us.

Nevertheless, Giacometti is dissatisfied. He could win the match promptly simply by deciding that he has won. But he can't make up his mind and keeps putting off his decision from hour to hour, from day to day. Sometimes, during the course of a night's work, he is ready to acknowledge his victory; by morning everything has been shattered. Is he afraid of the boredom that lurks beyond his triumph, the boredom that beset Hegel after he had imprudently stapled together his system? Or perhaps matter seeks revenge. Perhaps the infinite divisibility that he eliminated from his work

91

keeps cropping up between him and his goal. The end is in sight, but to reach it he must improve.

Much has been done but now he must do *a little* better. And then *just a little* better still. The new Achilles will never catch the tortoise; a sculptor must in some way be the chosen victim of space — if not in his work, then in his life. But between him and us, there must always be a difference of position. He knows what he wanted to do and we don't; but we know what he has done and he doesn't. His statues are still largely incorporated in his flesh; he is unable to see them. Almost as soon as they are produced he goes on to dream of women that are thinner, taller, lighter, and it is through his work that he envisions the ideal by virtue of which he judges it imperfect. He will never finish simply because a man always transcends what he does.

"When I finish," he says, "I'll write, I'll paint, I'll have fun." But he will die before finishing. Are we right or is he right? He is right because, as Da Vinci said, it is not good for an artist to be happy. But we are also right — and ours is the last word. Kafka as he lay dying asked to have his books burned and Dostoevski, during the very last moments of his life, dreamed of writing a sequel to *The Brothers Karamazov*. Both may have died dissatisfied, the former thinking that he would depart from the world without even making a mark on it and the latter that he had not produced anything good. And yet both were victors, regardless of what they might have thought.

Giacometti is also a victor, and he is well aware of this fact. It is futile for him to hoard his statues like a miser and to procrastinate, temporize and find a hundred excuses for borrowing more time. People will come into his studio, brush him aside, carry away all his works, including the plaster that covers his floor. He knows this; his cowed manner betrays him. He knows that he has won in spite of himself, and that he belongs to us.

INDEX